This is our time. This is our time to stand up and use our true power to make things right. How will we find the healthy, peaceful families, communities, and nations for which we long? How can we evolve from war consciousness to peace consciousness? It comes down to us. We're the peace. We're the ones. We're the peaceful world for which we long. We can no longer cling to the illusion that peace will somehow be delivered to us by leaders wiser and more powerful than we are. We're the wise and powerful ones. We will know the blessings of peace when we learn and practice the ways of peace.

*Susan Skog*

Other Books by Susan Skog

Embracing Our Essence:
Spiritual Conversations with Prominent Women

Radical Acts of Love:
How Compassion Is Transforming Our World

Depression:
What Your Body's Trying to Tell You

ABC's for Living

# PEACE IN OUR LIFETIME

Insights from the World's
Peacemakers

by
Susan Skog

Foreword by Thich Nhat Hanh

Published by Cliffrose Communications, LLC
Colorado

Cliffrose Communications, LLC
Fort Collins, CO

Web site to order books: www.cliffrosebooks.com
Web site to contact Susan Skog: www.susanskog.com

For information about special discounts for bulk purchases, please
e-mail jim@cliffrosebooks.com or phone 970-226-3014

Printed in the United States of America
July 2004

Cover design by Sue Sell, Periwinkle Design
Cover photo by Portraits by Betsy

Library of Congress Control Number 2004109696

ISBN 0-9758696-0-4

# Acknowledgments

To my husband, Jim, and sons, Jeff and Evan, my love and thanks for believing in this project and helping me bring it to life. I extend my gratitude to these wonderful people, whose inspiration and work were woven into this book: My agent, Chris Tomasino, for seeing the wisdom in my message and helping me crystallize it; Lynn Kendall, Mark Sloniker, Colleen Crosson, and all the wondrous people at Fort Collins Unity for your joy; Faith Brandt and Kathy Kenney for the solace and strength of your yoga instruction; Martha Goodell for your beautiful editing, support, and creativity in the early stages of the project; Teresa Funke for your friendship, exquisite publishing guidance, and support in taking this leap of faith; Tracy Ekstrand for your extraordinary, sage editing—and humor—at just the right moment; Harvey Tillis for your web design perfection; Margot Slosson for your incredible support in the critical, final stretch; Jessica Everly and Bryden Spencer for your support of our boys and family; Sue Sell for your beautiful cover design and playful creativity; and Portraits by Betsy for a fun photo shoot.

Lots of love to my parents, Bob and Vivian Stuekerjuergen, and my friends Beth Knees, Jackie Mahan, Margueritte Meier, Susan Mead, Jessica Saperstone, Cynthia Slosson, and Ann Swanson. You all know how long this book took to emerge, and I'm grateful for your understanding and friendship during it all.

Finally, I express my deep appreciation to all the peacemakers who took the time to pause and reflect on their work. They show that the world is a shining and beautiful place.

# Table of Contents

# Foreword

*To some, peace and nonviolence are synonymous with passivity and weakness. In truth, practicing peace and nonviolence is far from passive. To practice peace, to make peace alive in us, is to actively cultivate understanding, love, and compassion, even in the face of misperception and conflict. Practicing peace, especially in times of war, requires courage.*

## My Dear Friends,

Violence, hatred, and despair are not only coming to you from the outside; they are coming from the inside. Our real enemies today are our own anger, our own violence, and our own discrimination and fear.

We have to go home to ourselves and listen to ourselves to become mindful, to be aware of what is going on. When you come home to yourself, you will be available to help others. If we can first practice taking good care of ourselves, our feelings and our emotions, we create zones of peace.

If you have peace and safety, others will also have peace and safety. And if you don't have peace and safety, others won't, either.

In our consciousness, we store many positive seeds of wisdom, understanding, compassion, and joy. We also store many negative seeds of pain, anger, despair, violence, and craving. These seeds are all in our consciousness, which is like the basement of our house.

It depends on how we live our daily lives whether these seeds become stronger or weaker. Every time a negative seed is watered, that seed will manifest. We have to be very careful in handling our seeds. If we don't live mindfully, we will continue to water the seeds of anger, despair, craving, and fear several times a day. Then they want to manifest all the time. And when they manifest all the time, you suffer.

It is possible to come home to your pain and sorrow with the practice of mindfulness. But you are afraid. You are used to being overwhelmed by your fear and despair.

You are trying so hard to prevent these strong seeds of anger and despair and fear and craving from manifesting in your culture by consumption, by staying so busy so the blocks of fear and anger and pain have no chance to come up.

You practice suppressing the fear and despair in you by watching TV, turning on the phone, picking up a magazine, and choosing unmindful consumption. Most of us try to run away from our suffering within by the way we consume. This is why they can sell things to you. Sometimes you need drugs and alcohol because the pain is so immense in you.

But we can stop running away from ourselves and transform our despair and suffering inside. Your energy of mindfulness is your ally to embrace your pain tenderly. Then you can understand the nature of your pain. You can transform and remove the violence, anger, and fear in you by practicing mindful breathing and walking.

You can practice by saying, "Breathing in, I know my anger is in me. Breathing out, I can take care of my anger now."

With the energy of mindfulness, you can recognize and embrace your anger and fear. There is no fighting going on.

If we can breathe and walk mindfully, we can embrace our anger and transform it. Then we will get relief. Every time we take a mindfulness bath, our anger will lose a little bit of strength.

Practice breathing mindfully every day. Sign a peace treaty with yourself to walk mindfully. Sign a peace treaty with your children and with your partner. Sign a peace treaty with your staircase to walk mindfully. "Breathing in, I am here. Breathing out, I am home. Breathing in, I am here. Breathing out, I am home. Breathing in, I am here. Breathing out, I am home."

Practice breathing in with each step. As you breathe mindfully, it will make you alive. It will bring you joy. It will make you happy.

To remove the violence and hate in the world, we also have to remove our wrong perceptions. Wrong perceptions are the foundation of violence, hate, fear, and despair.

Only the practice of compassionate listening can remove the wrong perceptions. When you listen compassionately to others, you are free of your wrong perceptions. And when you are free of wrong perceptions, understanding and love can make their way into your heart. You can restore communication with love and compassion.

I think America should go home to herself and listen to herself and recognize the suffering inside of America. There is fear. There is confusion. There is anger. There is violence. There are too many people in America who still believe they are objects of discrimination and social injustice.

It's my conviction that in America there are people who are capable of listening with deep compassion to the difficulties of others. If people can come together and voice their concerns strongly, offer their light to the whole nation, and show the path, that would be wonderful. If America can listen to the suffering of its own nation and repair the damage done to its own nation, America will inspire many people. That will show that America is capable of listening to the suffering of other nations.

We have to practice this mindfulness energy as people, as a city, as a nation. We have to be able to recognize, embrace, and transform our anger. The anger of one person can ruin them and their family. The anger of one nation can ruin other nations.

The first step is to come home to ourselves. You don't need to become a Buddha. You need to become yourself.

*Adapted with permission from Dharma Talk, Wisdom and Compassion in Action Conference, Estes Park, Colorado, September 2003.*

Thich Nhat Hanh is a Buddhist monk, poet, peace activist, and the author of *Creating True Peace, Being Peace,* and more than 100 other books. He was nominated by Martin Luther King Jr. for the Nobel Peace Prize.

# *Introduction*
# ASSUMING OUR POWER

W ho isn't longing for a calmer, saner world? Conflict across the earth and in our own back yards is making us war-weary people. We're all drained as bombings, ambushes, and hatred claim more lives in Iraq, the Middle East, everywhere in the world. We're all anxious as neighbors attack neighbors. As tensions glow hot in North Korea and Liberia. As adults hurt children, and children hurt each other.

Even when we're not physically in the crossfire of wars, we're still affected by them. Like people living downwind of nuclear test sites, we're contaminated by the radioactivity of conflict. We're bombarded by the fallout.

We weren't meant to live this way. We weren't meant to harm one another. Layered upon the unrest in our own lives, violence anywhere leaves us vulnerable. "When we prey on each other, something goes shockingly wrong," says Michael Nagler, author of *Is There No Other Way? The Search for a Nonviolent Future.*

We all deserve far, far better than this. And we long, more than ever before, for something greater. A critical mass of us has had enough. We need a new way. We're hungry for some signs of hope. We want a more peaceful world, for us and for our children.

Right now, an unprecedented number of us have been awakened, activated, and mobilized by these feelings. We are consciously reaching for nonviolent ways to resolve our conflicts, personal and political, individual and collective.

This is our time to make things right. This is our time to stand up and use our true power to create a change in our own lives and in the world. How will we find the healthy, peaceful families, communities, and nations for which we long? How can we evolve from war consciousness to peace consciousness? How can we move from the politics of cruelty to the politics of compassion?

When will we stop bloodying one another? How can our communities, even our own homes, be safe for our children? Is anywhere "safe" these days?

It has come down to us. We're the peace. We're the ones. Peace is, always has been, always will be up to you and me. We're the peaceful world for which we long.

We can't live the illusion that peace will somehow be delivered to us by leaders wiser and more powerful than we are. We're the wise and powerful ones. Peace won't just magically descend on us like snowfall in the night. We will know the blessings of peace when we learn and practice the ways of peace. "Nobody is going to do it for us," says Arn Chorn Pond, a Vietnamese refugee-turned-peacemaker whose entire family was killed in Vietnam in 1975. "You and I have to make choices every step we go in our life."

Peace is a conscious decision, says Susan Collin Marks, a peacemaker who helped South Africa make its successful transition to democracy. "Just as we decide to wage war, we decide to make peace. It is true from the personal to the international. We make the decision to be angry and violent or not. We decide to make peace or not."

We choose peace. We choose peace each time we nurture loving, humane relationships. We choose peace when we disarm ourselves, stop the wars raging within ourselves, and solve our conflicts more creatively. We choose peace when we elect leaders who choose peace.

# Introduction

War and violence display a gross lack of imagination for something greater and more powerful. Using military action to destroy terror is "like hitting a fully mature dandelion with a golf club," says peacemaker John Paul Lederach. It only seeds more terrorism.

We choose peace when we awaken to this truth, stay vigilant, and see the possibilities for change. We choose peace each time we stop supporting the forces that profit from violence and support the forces of peace and compassion.

We also choose peace powerfully when we simply sit, breathe, relax, and stay openhearted—often challenging in today's whirling, angry world. "Having a cup of tea, I stop the war," is a wonderful Zen saying.

No matter how we express it individually, you and I represent the peace we seek. Join the force of peace growing and swelling all over the world. No matter where you look, many, many people are rising up and working for peace.

They're championing humane policies in their communities, calling for better conflict-resolution and peacemaking in our schools, helping enemies reconcile, and creating more nurturing homes. They're rejecting violent media and consumer products and making socially conscious purchases, expressing their power through their purchases.

Join this force. Fuel this force. Watch this force transform our culture as we know it. Don't allow your anger to do more harm. If we're choked with anger or divisiveness, we can't use our voices to call for change, and we send out "a set of vibrations that is just causing more war," author Ram Das says. We have to realize our power to choose something greater.

Much is at stake. This is an amazing time. Let's do something unstoppable. Let's work hard and engage strong emotions and actions not to fight with those who love conflict but to create a better society that lifts up all of us sharing this earth. "We're not trying to fight the old system. We're trying to build a new one," says Marks.

Collectively, we're writing a new chapter in our evolution, in our humanity. And there is much to be hopeful about. If you tune into morning television, you can get a scalding dose of violence to go with your steaming coffee, but beyond the piped-in hysteria, there is an incredibly hopeful story playing out all over the world. That is the story this book illuminates and celebrates.

It's a story that each of us can help direct, produce, participate in, and broadcast all over the earth. Even as people pour out their fury and despair on battlefields, crowded marketplaces, and corporate workplaces, the outpouring for peace is far, far greater.

This is a story not shared by mainstream media or the powers that glorify violence. This is the story we must share with one another, wherever we are, e-mail by e-mail, conversation by conversation, heart to heart. We have never seen so many people, from Somalia to San Francisco, Detroit to Dublin, working to sow peace. In the spring of 2003, more than 12 million people in over 700 cities in 60 countries on every continent went to the streets to call for peace.

This story builds as millions more gather in locations around the world, on the Internet, in classrooms, at conferences, rallies, and retreats to explore, celebrate and call for peace. So many people are rising up that we can no longer keep track of their numbers. But we can sense it in our souls and in our will.

Epic change is flowing across the earth as never before in the form of citizen voices, actions, and organizations. "Never before in the history of the world has there been a global, visible, public, viable, open dialogue and conversation about the legitimacy of war," says Dr. Robert Muller, former assistant secretary-general of the United Nations.

The force for something greater than war is so vast that the *New York Times* dubbed it "the world's other superpower."

Celebrate this. Be grateful for this. As teachers unite with business leaders, unite with schoolchildren, unite with conflict-resolution workers, unite with grandmothers, teachers, CEOs, health workers, lawyers, and countless others across our society, the web of peace keeps widening and growing. As an Ethiopian proverb says, "When spider webs unite, they can halt even a lion."

Even when global peace seems an impossible stretch, we can reach for and find harmony in our own lives. And the world, in those moments, tilts powerfully and inexorably toward greater peace.

And the truth is, peace has already chosen us. We already hold deep peace within us, if only we will access it. "Peace is present right here and now, in ourselves and everything we do and see," says Thich Nhat Hanh. "The question is whether or not we are in touch with it."

Just as we're responsible for our own happiness, we're responsible for our own peace. Even when others act aggressively, we have to actively stay calm and spread that peace. Even if, all around us, people act out their hatred and fear, we have to heal our anger so it doesn't lead us to wage war on others. "Peace is as much about getting the bombs out of our own hearts as out of the Pentagon budget," says peace educator and former *Washington Post* columnist Colman McCarthy.

Peace is freeing our hearts to burn with compassion, not hate. In our personal relationships or our connections with other countries, when we stop harming one another and begin to honor our precious connections as human beings—even when we disagree—we will have peaceful lives.

Peacemaking is not the exclusive domain of high-ranking politicians, mediators, or diplomats. We know now that we can't surrender our power in that way. We have to take responsibility mindfully and build a peaceful culture, beginning with our own thoughts and actions. We have to make our homes, schools, workplaces, and communities the Camp Davids at which we negotiate peace. We have to support politicians and other leaders who want peace as much as we do. We have to hold peace in our own lives. We need to stay hopeful.

All of this led me to gather inspiring, hope-filled stories from peacemakers, some of whom work in the hottest zones of conflict around the world. Despite the chaos they have seen and experienced, all still have high, high hopes for peace.

I talked with negotiators who meet with and create peace among trained-to-kill guerilla soldiers, combative freedom fighters, hostile workers, refugees, angry students, and devastated survivors of war.

These stories come from people like Arun Gandhi, who refused to hate the man who assassinated his grandfather, Mahatma Gandhi; Amber Amundson, whose husband was killed on September 11; William Ury, internationally known mediator; Kimmie Weeks, who was forced to flee Liberia and works now from America as a peacemaker; and Sherri Mandell, whose son was stoned to death in Palestine and who chose to sow peace in the Middle East.

Other stories come from people whose lives became enmeshed in more ordinary conflicts, from lawsuits to neighborhood feuds. They reclaimed their lives by choosing peace—and show how we can do the same.

Over and over, these peacemakers echo the same, hopeful message: The peace measures that calm chronic tensions all over the world are the same ones that can ease the conflicts in our own lives. And the minute we begin to apply these skills to our days, right where we are, we bring peace not just to ourselves but to our entire earth. We can know peace in our lifetime.

We can step into the role of peacemakers, whether that means listening respectfully to people we don't agree with, forgiving an enemy, or building communities based on the common good.

The choice is ours. It may be easier to be livid or depressed about the state of the world. It's all too easy to reel in horror at the arrogance and aggression of our government officials. Our own leaders have not only ignored our calls for peace but intentionally and recklessly chosen a more destructive path. At the same time, the media has routinely neglected to report the full cost and horror of war—financial, political, and spiritual—or document the power of those working for peace. Feeling angry about all of this is understandable.

But be mindful. Anger alone can't get us what we want. Bitterness can't bring soldiers safely home from military campaigns to their families or give them the support and healing they deserve. With anger alone, we can't turn away from aggression and arrogance. We need a better path, and we need our hearts and souls to remain grounded on that path.

We need to transform our anger into purpose and passion. Only then can we respond with greater conviction and move our culture and world to a higher level.

This is a watershed moment. These are the times to hold steady, breathe deeply, connect with our hearts, be smart, stay alert, and call on our true power. To have as powerful and as widespread an impact as we need, we'll need our homes and communities to stay grounded in hope and the possibility of healing.

As we do so, remember what seasoned peacemaker William Ury holds high: The majority of people living on the earth right now already know peace. We have for a long, long time. The majority of us are already resolving our conflicts nonviolently. We are already a sweeping force of peace.

We can keep this force alive in our own hearts and actions. We can hold, at our centers, the peace we want at the core of our world. We can focus on and amplify this light all over the earth.

"It is an exciting age, filled with hope. It is an age in which a new social order is being born. We stand today between two worlds—the dying old and the emerging new," Dr. Martin Luther King Jr. said. Some 40 years later, his words awaken us to our true greatness. "I speak as a citizen of the world," King said then. We can do the same now.

Many of us sense we were destined for this work. We feel we've been moving toward this moment for quite some time.

"We were made for these times," says author Clarissa Pinkola Estes. "Yes. For years, we have been learning, practicing, been in training for and just waiting to meet on this exact plane of engagement."

"I grew up on the Great Lakes and recognize a seaworthy vessel when I see one. Regarding awakened souls, there have never been more able crafts in the waters than there are right now across the world."

We've been learning more about our wholeness and our connection to everything else on earth. We've been learning that what unites all of us is much greater than what divides us. We've been raising our consciousness, so when peacemaker Sam Gbaydee Doe says, "I exist because you exist," we know exactly of what he speaks. We all exist because of and for each other.

Now, after September 11, his words make total, holy sense to us. Our very existence depends on the existence of all on earth.

We are of each other. Combat and violence of any kind destroy our wholeness. They threaten our existence. This knowledge, on an intuitive level, is speaking to people everywhere and giving them the courage to call out for peace.

Speak up for peace every day. Keep speaking up, even when it's intimidating or uncomfortable. "Our lives begin to end the day we become silent about things that matter," Dr. King said.

Imagine peace every day. Use your thoughts to create the kind of world for which you long. Dream of peace. Imagination is even greater than knowledge because imagination "circles the world," Albert Einstein said. And if anyone knew about how light could circle the globe, Einstein certainly did.

Remember how it feels to be happy and fulfilled. Visualize how your life will be different when peace grows among you and those you love. Imagine your neighborhood, school, church, synagogue, temple, workplace, and entire community cooperative and thriving. Imagine your country no longer warring with others. Imagine our reaching out and finding common ground and prosperity with other nations. Visualize yourself falling in love with the diversity, beauty, and wonder of people of other cultures.

# Introduction

Imagine how all of that will feel. Then imagine how great it will be not to fight with family members, co-workers, neighbors, bosses, and friends or neighbors around the world. Imagine. Believe in all of it. Believe, as Archbishop Desmond Tutu does, that anything war can do, peace can do better.

And now believe you can have everything of which you dream. "Dream. Dream. Dream. Be idealistic. Dream the world can be a better place. God is saying, 'Help me to realize my dream,'" Tutu says.

Believe that peace can happen. Peace will soothe our war-weary days as soon as we love the idea of living in harmony more than we love the idea of living in chaos. Peace can only be created by our wanting peace more than we want war.

Forgive; don't fight. Listen to the experiences of people who haven't had the blessings you have. Listen to their anger and their pain but don't return the same. Try to find some inherent, human connection to those who have harmed us and to those we have harmed. See how much we all long for the same things: secure homes, fulfilling work, healthy children, loving families, prosperity, and dreams fulfilled.

Can we become so expansive and loving that we no longer return cruelty with more cruelty? Can we become people of peace who can understand, transform, and heal suffering for the greater good of all?

There's a lot of talk about homeland security these days. We say we want homeland security so much we are willing to pay dearly for it. The peacemakers you'll meet in this book show that security, whether in our own homeland or the homelands of others on earth, will never, ever come from threats, intimidation, or violence. We can't bully our way to homeland security.

"The only lasting security," said Mahatma Gandhi, "is found in love."

True homeland security is rooted in nonviolence. If we harm others and create even more desperation, poverty, and misery, we breed more suicide bombers, more violence. We see that hourly.

21

We can only become secure when we care for others and ensure that they receive basic necessities and human rights, says Tutu. "There can be no real security for all until we ensure the conditions don't exist that make other people desperate and resentful," he says.

Ultimately, security for ourselves, our families, our homes—and for those around the world—is found in well-ordered, strong, loving relationships among people who care so deeply for one another that they will never hurt each other. Peace comes down to our wanting better lives for ourselves and those sharing the earth with us.

"None of the people that I work with want to be in the messes that they're in. They want to find ways that their communities and their families and their children can live a more healthy and pleasant life," says peacemaker John Paul Lederach. "Families and communities and nations that are healthy are what peacebuilding is all about."

May this book serve as a steppingstone to the peace we all crave. Thank you to the courageous peacemakers laying down this path, person by person.

These turbulent times are testing all of us. They shake us to the core. But they're also exposing us to our core selves—our beliefs, shadows, and possibilities. And that is a valuable gift.

They've opened up an unprecedented opportunity for change. "I personally believe a doorway has opened for our evolution, and we are being presented with a number of gifts and opportunities," says peacemaker Louise Diamond.

Speaking after the United States began to bomb Afghanistan in 2001, Diamond said, "I don't mean to slight the tragedy of the events we are living through. People are suffering greatly in many places and in many ways. Yet if we can draw out and act on the lessons that are available to us, we can use this war as a jumping-off place for greater peace. We can set a different, positive pattern for our collective future."

# Introduction

We've seen and felt enough violence. We need more tenderness, stability, and joy. We need more hope. We need one another. "We are each other's harvest...We are each other's magnitude and bond," says poet Gwendolyn Brooks.

We can't just sing about peace on earth in our churches and schools, though that's a start. We have to carry the song of peace in our hearts wherever we go. We have to know how to hold the peace when the music stops.

We can't just send greeting cards calling for peace on earth each holiday season. Peace needs to become a passionate call in every season.

We bear the responsibility—and privilege—of putting an end to the wars in our own lives. We do have to bring terrorists, including those in our own culture, to justice, but we also have to do justice to our deep yearnings for peace.

Peace in our lifetime all comes down to our own choices, individual and collective. When the world splits open as it has, how do we respond? Do we set the intention to choose a peaceful response? Do we choose love?

David Potorti's world split open September 11 when his brother Jim died at the World Trade Center. After his brother's death, a quote from Samuel Johnson about choosing "the triumph of hope over experience" lingered in his mind.

"That quote continues to resonate with me. And I've come to the conclusion that, even following the events of September 11 that took my brother's life, I'm choosing hope over experience. I'm choosing peace over war. And I've come to another conclusion: If I can do it, so can you.

"I emphasize the word *choose* because we know our initial reaction to being attacked, to having loved ones lose their lives. Anger. Fear. Apprehension. This burning desire to strike back right away. We're only human. I don't pretend to be some kind of saint or to be speaking from a higher plane of consciousness. But I acknowledge having choices."

These times call on all of us to recognize and own our choices, and then to exercise the choices that serve the common good. We are part of a whole. We must nurture and protect the whole of life, here and around the world. We must do this for our own lives and the lives of our children.

In a stormy world, one of the most calming and powerful actions we can take is to "stand up and show your soul," author Clarissa Pinkola Estes says. What a magnificent idea. We can stand up and show our souls by learning the ways of love and peace. We can capture our fierce strength of heart until wars no longer exist.

This is noble, beautiful work. It brings us to the very best of ourselves. Yes, we can have peace in our lifetime. And, yes, it begins with me, with you, with each of us.

*One*

# BELIEVING IN PEACE

*A* t key moments in U.S. history, we've often been surprised by "the sudden coming to life of a flame we thought extinguished," said Howard Zinn in 1994 in *You Can't Be Neutral on a Moving Train*. Ten years later, we're witnessing such a flame coming to life not only in our country but around the world.

Many people are initially surprised at how swiftly this flame for peace has leapt to consciousness. They can't offer a logical explanation for the numbers of people clamoring overnight for a more humane way to solve our conflicts.

What Zinn observed a decade ago holds true now: "We are surprised because we don't see that beneath the surface of the present there is always the human material for change: the suppressed indignation, the common sense, the need for community, the love of children, the patience to wait for the right moment to act in concert with others. These are the elements that spring to the surface when a movement appears in history."

What's causing you to rise up for change? Was it the stark moments of September 11 when everything shifted? Is it the draining unrest of the Iraq War? Perhaps this global conflict, layered upon the conflict in your own life, is simply more than you want to live with.

Whatever the reason, the psychic sea change in our culture is pointing to the fact that more and more people appear to be willing to end the wars within themselves and with others.

So how do we begin? We start first with our intention. If we really want a more peaceful world, we have to set the intention to be peaceful people who, one by one, mirror the peaceful culture we want to create. We intend to display cooperation and harmony in our interactions so those values will spread in our own worlds and across the world.

We've simply not set the intention often enough or invested well enough in peace. Peace is often back-burnered, kind of an afterthought when things get out of control. Peace is regarded as an elective course, not the main lesson for us all. Why don't we create more of an opening for peace in our communities? Why do local and state governments, school districts, corporations, and hospitals spend millions of dollars on disputes after they rage out of control instead of investing in ways to prevent them?

Why don't our students study and discuss peacemaking more? Why do they learn who started, fought, and died in every major conflict but very little about who healed conflicts over time?

Even more importantly, why do we give up so easily on peaceful solutions to conflict? Why do we often feel it's not even worth the effort? Is it that we believe fighting is always, sadly, inevitable? Has chronic conflict become such a constant in our lives that we're resigned to the idea that it's just a predictable part of life?

In setting our intention to hold peace every day, we can learn much from people who've worked to secure peace in the most violent areas on earth and often succeeded. Here are some ways to begin to hold peace in your life. These steps are being used by peacemakers all over the world:

# Remember What Peace and Harmony Feel Like

Recall a time when all felt peaceful in your life. Remember how great that felt. Remember how much better it was to live without chronic tension and fighting. How did you spend your time? What did you enjoy about that period in your life?

If ongoing conflict consumes your days, it's easy to forget how great peace feels, especially when we look at the barrage of bleak media images these days. "I prefer to believe we are on the brink of a Great Remembering, a time when America's prosperity allows us to reconsider what matters most to us," says Peter Forbes, author of *The Great Remembering*.

Let's help each other remember what really matters. Let's set the intention to desire, speak for, and reach for peace in our own back yards. Let's remember that the world's becoming more chaotic or more peaceful depends on us.

Let's also remember our connection to one another, knowing that whatever hurts one of us hurts us all, and whatever heals one of us heals us all. Being conscious of this will help us keep our intentions high, creating a zone of peace around us. "If you are yourself at peace, then there is at least some peace in the world. Then share your peace with everyone, and everyone will be at peace," Thomas Merton said.

Peace comes when we remember that, through this bond of our relationships, we deliver peace or shatter it. It starts with our own intention to remember that war isn't inevitable, that we don't have to hurt others who hurt us.

John Paul Lederach has seen peace spring up in war zones when people set the intention for peace and remember how great peace feels. A professor at Eastern Mennonite University's Institute for Justice and Peacebuilding, Lederach has seen the Great Remembering for peace rise up in the ugliest war zones. He is a seasoned peacemaker and the author of numerous peace books, including *Can't We All Just Get Along? The Journey toward Reconciliation*.

For decades, he has spent time in and studied cultures worn down by chronic fighting that still somehow manage to successfully carve out peace, at least for a time. The people there, against all odds, pushed violence to the margins of their society after they remembered how much they wanted peace and set the intention for it.

Part of that remembering was knowing that their welfare— and their children's—was deeply tied to everyone around them, even to those who may have hurt them horribly. Once they remembered that, they could better remember how to reach for peace, Lederach says. They could finally look above the narrow, ugly conflict in front of them. They began to see a wider, more hopeful horizon of possibilities. They finally knew that, for the sake of future generations, they had to do the right thing, Lederach says. They had to stop fighting.

"These people don't so much have a grandiose theory or theology to explain what they're doing, as a recognition that their family's and their children's futures are connected to a large degree to the future of the families in the community on the other side of the divide."

With that kind of "moral imagination" for a new future, with that kind of opening for peace then visible, people can push violence to the fringe of their communities, even while still living with it, because they see themselves as part of a web of relationships, even with their enemies, Lederach says. They work to strengthen that web, not the violence.

Lederach has seen this happen in Columbia, where intense fighting has raged for decades between government forces, paramilitary groups, guerilla movements, drug lords, and other armed factions. He has heard of groups of rural farmers, in areas hotly contested by armed groups, who still set their deep intention for peace, knowing that they want something better for themselves, their families, and future generations.

"One small group of rural farmers had a candid talk about what they could do to keep from getting overrun by one side or the other. For decades, their choices were very limited. One armed group would take over and say to the farmers, 'You can stay and join us, or you can leave...You can join the enemy, but if you do, we will come after you.'"

One of the Columbian farmers remembered that he and his fellow farmers could make other choices, Lederach says. He took a leap of faith one day. He saw the opening, the consensus for peace, and before a gathering of about 500 farmers, the man vowed that he would not fight. He urged others to join him.

"The farmer said, 'We will die before we will kill. We will first speak to every armed group and pursue relentless dialogue. No one will come with weapons.' His speech was so memorable that people two years later could still recite it from memory," Lederach says.

Sticking to their intention for nonviolence, the group of Columbian farmers chose key principles for their group to create zones of nonviolence. "They achieved quite significant progress by simply standing together as a community and engaging in dialogue with all the armed forces. It's really an extraordinary story....In the long run, the capacity to give people a voice and move out of cycles of violence doesn't come through some miraculous formula only a few people are involved in. It requires an enormous number of people on a day-to-day basis, living right in the middle of these situations, often within close range of people who have harmed them, reconciling at the core."

## Find the Opening for a Consensus for Peace

Before peace breaks out, events, people, and consciousness need to shift so something new can be born. The miracle of South Africa, for instance, came about "when the leadership decided to seek a negotiated end to apartheid, when civil society rolled up its sleeves and joined in, and when the majority of people showed their willingness to 'forgive but not forget,'" says peacemaker Susan Collin Marks. "It took vision, hard work, and a leap of faith to get there, and in just four years, South Africa ended apartheid and held peaceful, democratic elections."

This "consensus for peace," as Marks calls it, signals that the time is ripe to act in concert with others and take the possibility for peace further.

In resolving your personal conflicts, look for such moments in your own life. See if you can sense a moment when everything seems to be aligning to allow you to ease tensions easily and gracefully. Maybe your attitude has softened or you simply remember how much you want to stop fighting. Maybe the individual you are fighting with has come forward with an apology. Look for those doorways to cooperative solutions.

Marks remembers how magical it was when enough people at all levels in South Africa set the vast intention for peace—a consensus for peace—that ultimately carried South Africa "across the abyss of self-destruction to the realm of hope." Marks is the executive vice president of Search for Common Ground, a nonprofit organization that promotes nonviolent, cooperative solutions to conflict around the world. A former journalist, she captured her experience in helping South Africa's process of transformation from apartheid in her book *Watching the Wind: Conflict Resolution during South Africa's Transition to Democracy.*

She writes of how, amazingly, the opening for peace emerged when South Africa's apartheid regime agreed to negotiate with the African National Congress, and the ANC agreed to negotiate with the government. "In one of the great paradoxes of our time, a pariah country whose government had legalized racism, divided its people into master and servant classes according to color, and consigned black people to lives of squalor and hopelessness created a multicultural peacemaking model for the world. From the terrible mess of apartheid, something new and beautiful was trying to be born."

Growing up in South Africa during apartheid, Marks was primed to become a peacemaker. But a specific moment in time signaled the opening for her to take her own intention deeper.

"Growing up under apartheid had a huge impact on me, more than for many, because my mother was deeply conscious and an anti-apartheid activist. She came from a humanitarian perspective, and she couldn't bear what was happening to others. Through my mother, I was exposed to a consciousness that was both spiritual and political.

"But because of my mother's work, I was also singled out as 'other.' I was sometimes ostracized by and isolated from other children. It was risky to associate with us because of what she was doing.

"My mother did her work for about 10 years. The government stopped her by threatening to ban her if she didn't voluntarily stop. Banning, which was decided without trial and lasted five years, meant a six p.m. to six a.m. curfew, reporting to the police station once or twice a day, restriction to the local municipal area, no meetings with more than one other person, and a range of other restrictions.

"This was unacceptable, because my mother was caring for her own mother, who lived 700 miles away and was terminally ill. We children were at boarding school, and my mother was under a lot of pressure from my father to give up her work. It was a cruel dilemma. My mother stopped what she was doing, and 18 months later she developed the cancer, which ultimately killed her."

When Marks was in her 30s, she was married, living in London, and still holding a space for peace through her work as a journalist and filmmaker, where she explored issues like poverty and at-risk youth. When her parents died, she went back to South Africa to tie up the loose threads of their lives. While there, she happened to hear about an organization that promoted dialogue between different communities in South Africa. Suddenly everything shifted. Her moment had unfolded.

"As I read about this organization, something resonated in me that was earthshaking. I sat in my bath that night, and tears poured down my face into the bath water. I knew I would have to give up my life in England. I knew I would have to come back to South Africa, roll up my sleeves, and engage.

"It was a very powerful moment, and it has profoundly shaped my life since then. I discovered that my life purpose was to help bring peace and peace consciousness into the world, to bring the spiritual and political together. That is what I am here to do."

Soon after, Marks ended her marriage, got a graduate degree in international relations, and moved to South Africa. She became one of hundreds of peacemakers working to ensure the transition from apartheid to what was called "the new South Africa." During that incredible process, as she worked with people on all sides of the conflict, Marks discovered the power of holding the intention for peace within herself.

"I believe that we have to start with ourselves. The critical thing is to be true to who we are, to be in integrity. That is how we build trust. When we are able to sit wholly in ourselves, then we are able to sit with a calm center with others....My instinct is to embrace all that is happening and make it all work for peace....I learned that, as a peacemaker, I could hold open the space for peace—but that it had to start within me.

"I had to be willing to be spacious within myself and, at times, allow what was happening happen without trying to stop or change it. There were also times when I needed to dive in as a catalyst to support the process of transformation. The key is to know the difference, which comes through intuition, experiences, and all the things that we learn as we grow."

While the top leaders negotiated South Africa's future, multiple stakeholders from the bottom up, including the religious and business sectors, trade unions, and the community, set about creating change and building peace on the ground. "When people at the top and bottom make a commitment to peace rather than to their side of the conflict, they create a constituency for peace. That constituency for peace then can stand up against the forces, the extremists from all sides, who are against peace."

We are going through a dramatic transformation now, in our own lives and in the life of the world, Marks says. Across the world, significant numbers of people are mobilizing for the nonviolent resolution of conflicts, she believes. We can build such an international constituency for peace.

"I believe a massive shift in consciousness is under way right now, and the turmoil and chaos we're seeing in the world represent the unrest that happens when old systems are dying but new ones have not yet been born. Rather than fighting the old system, we need to focus on building a new one that is so attractive that it will, literally, attract the energy from the old in a continuing process."

Even though the world is in deep crisis, it is evolving in an essentially positive direction, Marks says. Each generation is learning from the previous generation. "I have great respect for young people who are now bringing more consciousness and growth through than we were able to manage. That is how I believe evolution works."

Deepening the shift in consciousness requires each of us to hold the intention for peace, Marks says. "I believe we all can do it. It is essential. The only way we can make peace is for each of us to be the peace we want to see. The greatest contribution we can make is in how we live our everyday lives. If we choose to live our lives caring for ourselves, each other, and the planet, then we make a choice for peace.

"Peace is generated by the way we live our lives in relationship with our families and communities. We need to live a very conscious life so that we don't contribute to the pain of the world in our everyday activities.

"We can choose to contribute to the beauty of the world through our interactions with other human beings. We have a choice to live our lives from a place of fear or a place of love. With fear, we constrict and alienate ourselves and close down, but with love, we expand and embrace and touch each other. These are the choices we can make…It is very simple."

# Hold the Peace in Ordinary Moments

In our daily routines, something radically new takes shape when we signal that we intend to stay peaceful in our hearts no matter what happens around us. A new chain of events is set in motion, and the peace we hold in our being is "caught" by others and lifts them, as well, to a higher place. In the moment that we extend our grace, the world becomes more liberated and more luminous.

Before you head out the door each morning, drive to work, and walk into your office, state your intention to hold peace. This is a power you bring to whomever or whatever you touch. Then with every conversation, every choice, every disagreement, try to stay calm and commit to looking for a peaceful solution.

Divine opportunities to hold peace often come through regular moments, like our daily phone calls, as Natalie Wieseltier discovered. Wieseltier, an Israeli, called a friend on her mobile phone one day, but she dialed the wrong number. Instead, she connected with a man named Jihad—a Palestinian.

Wieseltier could have done any number of things, including hanging up. But she chose to stay on the line and talk. Her number was recorded on Jihad's cell phone, and he later called her back. They shared some more. Eventually, Wieseltier talked with other members of Jihad's family, too. Now, after every terrorist attack, Jihad and his relatives call Wieseltier to make sure she's OK.

Wieseltier was so moved by what happened that she decided to see if a hotline could be created for other Palestinians and Israelis to connect by phone. The Hello Shalom–Hello Salaam hotline was set up through the Forum for Bereaved Families, a group of Israelis and Palestinians whose loved ones had been killed in the Israeli-Palestinian conflict but who still believed peace was possible.

The hotline was announced in ads that read: "Two years have passed without our speaking to each other. You get shot at, and we get bombs exploding on us. We're angry and we're in pain, and the other side certainly feels the same. It's time to put an end to this."

The hope for Hello Shalom–Hello Salaam was that, if ordinary citizens could reach out and speak to one another, holding fast to the intention to stay peaceful, peace could grow throughout the Middle East. Some 40,000 phone calls later, peace is indeed spreading from this extraordinary "accident."

In addition to speaking to one another, people have left hundreds of voice messages. Israeli Miriam Inbal left this message: "We are all people and want the best for our children and grandchildren. We have the power to make a change." She was in a car with friends when she got her first response, from a 28-year-old father of two living near a part of Egypt packed with poverty-stricken Palestinian refugee camps. "He asked me to speak to his two children," Inbal said. "He wanted them to know that Jews are not monsters."

All from a wrong number. The power of one of us staying calm and focused on peace can never be underestimated.

## Realize That You Can Always Choose Peace

Every moment is a great moment for choosing peace. Is this your moment? Do you sense that you might finally heal a stubborn disagreement that's resisted healing until now? Could this be your chance to help peace rise in the world through your daily choices?

Peter Forbes points out that a butterfly's disturbance of the air in East Africa can lead to a storm system six weeks later in New England. We are this intimately, elegantly connected. "The same stream of life that runs through the world runs through my veins night and day and dances in rhythmic measure," says Tabindranath Tagore.

So if you and I dance in greater kindness and compassion, this can tilt us all toward a more humane world, as it did in South Africa. Peace unfolds the same way everywhere.

It really is up to us. We're all in charge of the next chapter on earth. What will we create? Something just as unsettled and chaotic? Will we continue to let the anger in our own hearts stoke the fires in the rest of the world? Or are we ready to script something more hopeful? If so, here's our moment.

It's true that, inside us, we all also have the longing to fight. And there are always people willing to go there with us. There always will be. If we give into that impulse, if we water the seeds of violence, as Thich Nhat Hanh says, we grow an ugly garden. But we also carry the impulse to live more nobly and sow peace, and that impulse we can water.

Use your thoughts wisely. Understand that your thoughts have power, says Dr. Christiane Northrup.

"Thoughts have a tendency to become their physical equivalent. This is one of the fundamental laws of the universe. Another is the law of attraction, which states that 'like attracts like.'....It is impossible to create peace and harmony if you're pushing against war. It's impossible to create peace and harmony if you're condemning George Bush, Dick Cheney, Colin Powell, et al. You don't have to agree with them, but realize that you'll be contributing to the energy that creates war if you assume an 'embattled' mentality concerning them."

Each of us matters greatly in the convictions, intentions, and consciousness we create in the world. Commit to peaceful thoughts and intentions. Plant a garden of greater stability and resilience.

When we get clear that peace is what we desire with all our hearts, we bring heaven not just to our part of the earth but to the entire world. We all feel the impact of one person's living peace. One person can set in motion a new creation that captures all our collective hopes, passions, energies, and visions.

What are you willing to set in motion? How do we begin, especially if too much around us appears anything but peaceful?

## Set the Intention for Peace in Your Own Home

By living consciously and reaching for peace in our own homes, we can anchor peace powerfully—even when global peace feels daunting. This story shows how one woman was able to do that:

"By the time I was a teenager, my house felt full of discord as my siblings rebelled against the strict edicts of my father, a military career officer," says Mary Bahus-Meyer.

"We were raised to have a strong sense of values and work ethic and to stand up for our beliefs—as long as those beliefs didn't disagree with my parents'."

Not surprisingly, harmony was hard to come by as Bahus-Meyer began to speak her own truth and question her parents' values and rules. Her questioning made her father even angrier because he wasn't used to anyone's challenging his decisions. "As a military man, my father was used to giving orders and seeing people jump."

By the time she was 17, the fighting was so great that Bahus-Meyer left home. "I felt it was better for everyone if I wasn't there anymore. I left home thinking, 'I'm never coming back. I can't pretend to be someone I'm not.'"

But before her 18th birthday, Bahus-Meyer was in a car accident and broke her collarbone. Because she was still a minor, she was forced to move back in with her parents. It was time for some personal "housecleaning" before that could happen, she concluded.

"I knew I had to make a decision. I knew that this time I wanted living at home to be different and better. I made a conscious decision to learn skills that would allow me to get along, handle my feelings, and still be who I was."

Bahus-Meyer started attending a transcendental meditation class. She learned how to calm her spirit and be more at peace with herself. She discovered yoga and ways to speak her truth authentically without being argumentative.

After she moved back home, she began to meditate in the morning and evening, which initially caused even more friction with her parents. "My parents were very much against it. They thought meditation was weird, 'wu-wu' stuff."

But determined, Bahus-Meyer began to hitchhike to her weekly meditation training. Within months, her parents noticed a definite change in their daughter.

She was able to voice her opinions calmly without being argumentative. In conversations with her father, she was more reflective and able to step back a moment and select words that still expressed how she felt but in a less threatening manner. "I saw that we could both be right in our own way. I told him that we just saw things differently. I learned how to be less reactive, take deep breaths, and keep the peace when we talked."

Within a few months, even though they still didn't understand what meditation was, her parents respected her need to practice it, Bahus-Meyer remembers. They began to create a quiet space in the family for her to meditate each day, which wasn't always easy with three other children. Learning meditation and new ways of easing the conflicts in her home helped her take ownership of her life, says Bahus-Meyer. "It helped us live in peace under the same roof."

Years later, married and the mother of a young daughter, Bahus-Meyer and her parents, now in their 70s, have a healthier relationship. "They are both practicing tai chi and learning about meditation. My mother said, 'Now I understand why you meditate.'"

Anytime people ask themselves, "How can I affect peace in the world?" it always has to come back to the self, Bahus-Meyer says. "If I am not taking care of my feelings, my body, my spirituality, how can I affect anyone else's? If we love ourselves, then we can channel that out to the world."

## Be Bold—Be Brave—Inspire Others

Howard Zinn says that people "want change but feel powerless, alone, do not want to be the blade of grass that sticks up above the others, and is cut down. They wait for a sign from someone else who will make the first move, or the second. And at certain times in history, there are intrepid people who take the risk that, if they make that first move, others will follow quickly enough to prevent their being cut down. And if we understand this, we might make that first move."

One person's intention to stand for peace, to set something new in motion, to make that first move has often changed the course of history. One person's rising up for something greater can totally realign the world as we know it. One such person, a Polish woman, set the intention for peace at just the right moment during Poland's solidarity movement.

When Polish workers felt imprisoned by communism and unfair labor practices, they decided to break free peacefully. Using the principles of Gandhi and Martin Luther King Jr., a group of Gdansk shipyard workers, including Lech Walesa, resolved to walk off their jobs and strike but to stay in the factories as a force of nonviolent solidarity.

They knew that, by staying in the factories instead of going into the streets or to their homes, they stood a greater chance of keeping the protest peaceful. They coached each other on how to stay calm and not engage in fights with the police, knowing they could win if they held steady.

It takes each of us to hold steady when something old is being shattered and something new is emerging. It takes individuals we rarely ever hear about, like Alina Pienkowska, a soft-spoken single mother. Her intention for peace and her intuition—at just the right time—tipped the balance for the solidarity movement.

From the windows of her apartment, Pienkowska watched the strike begin. She realized immediately that the state security agencies would cut the phone lines to the shipyards to keep the strike secret from the world, so she rushed to call friends. They, in turn, quickly alerted Western reporters, ensuring the news would spread far beyond Poland. Now the rest of the world could watch, hope, and deepen the intention for peace.

Two days later, Pienkowska joined her fellow strikers in the shipyard. Again she turned the events toward unprecedented peace. By then, workers from many smaller factories and government establishments in the region had also joined the strike, so solidarity ranks had spread far beyond the shipyard.

But when the shipyard management offered the strikers a considerable raise, the workers accepted. They gladly called an end to the strike, and thousands of shipyard workers rushed to the gates to go home to their families.

Pienkowska was horrified. She realized that, if those workers left, they would leave the remaining strikers at other factories alone and vulnerable.

Again she acted instinctively. She managed to shut one gate, grabbed a loudspeaker, and passionately pleaded with the workers to stay and maintain the strike. She called on them to take responsibility for the other strikers, who were left exposed. She urged them to stay steady and see the strike through for all of Poland.

Most of the workers headed home, but enough lingered—or came back that night upon the urging of their wives—that the shipyard filled up once again. Within days, 50,000 workers and 22 factories had joined the strike. By the ninth day, the strike committee spoke for half a million workers, and the communists' grip was broken.

The whole world watched Poland's glorious arc toward a new peace. We all felt inspired—If peace was possible there, it was possible anywhere. Pienkowska went on to become a senator and was active in local politics and health issues until she died in 2002.

She showed that even one person holding the intention for peace can start or contribute to a movement and keep it alive. It all begins with our intention.

# WHAT MORE CAN YOU DO?

- ## Recognize That Your Intention Is Powerful

We aren't insignificant. Our personal peace and the peace of the entire world are linked. Our responses in everyday moments aren't trivial or disconnected from others. Our own peace and the peace of the world are impacted by what we each choose in these daily encounters. We can set in motion either great beauty or something less. The peacemaking organization Everyday Gandhis works to heal conflicts and create peaceful communities in Africa. Be an Everyday Gandhi in your own part of the world.

- ## Take 30 Seconds to Visualize Peace

We attract peace with our thoughts. We use our thoughts all the time to dream of and attract a new home, job, or relationship. We can do the same with peace. Spend 30 seconds each day creating a virtual reality of what peace would look and feel like, says Dr. Christiane Northrup. Imagine, for instance, all the world's leaders healthy and vibrant and cooperating beautifully. Imagine all our soldiers back home and reunited with their families. Imagine a global village in which all of us can travel freely and joyously, with understanding and acceptance of each other's cultures. Choose to imagine what peace most looks like to you.

- ## Practice Breathing to Peace

To hold the peace, practice being peace. At different points in your day, stop and breathe deeply until you feel calmer and more peaceful. Start one moment at a time. Start now. As you read this page, pause and breathe in your desire to connect with your peaceful self. Keep breathing until you feel calm, knowing that all is well. During the day, if you can stay aligned with your breath, you will have a solid foundation, a resting place on which you can depend. Then when you find yourself on unexpected ground, thrown out of your comfort zone, you can breathe in, stay grounded, and remind yourself that you are peace. You hold and extend peace. You can access that peace when suddenly someone you've resented is standing right in front of you at the grocery checkout line. It will support you when a co-worker loses his cool and verbally attacks you. You can access this inner peace whenever something unsettling or threatening happens. You already carry peace inside, and it is a formidable force.

Whenever we have those raw moments, whenever we have to make a decision, we can take a stand, right in the middle of what feels uncomfortable—even painful—and not be thrown off balance. "Breathing in, I am solid. Breathing out, I am free", says Thich Nhat Hanh.

- **Stabilize Your Organization**

In our workplaces, whenever even one of us sets the intention to escalate conflict, the world becomes more vulnerable. We all feel it. Look at how the rage of just a few can unsettle and destabilize many. So when others want to gossip, choose to disconnect. If others want to be divisive or combative, choose not to participate. If your co-workers seem to have no hope for the future, offer some possibility for change. Listen to the story of someone who feels invisible.

- **Take a Peace Inventory of Your Life**

How peaceful are you on a day-to-day basis? How often and under what circumstances do you tend to lose your peace and get frustrated or furious? When do things seem too bleak to hold onto hope?

Become conscious of how and when you start to let your energy be drained. Look back honestly at times you have fueled instead of calmed arguments in your relationships, workplace, and community.

Only you can get clear with yourself about what needs to shift for you to have more peace right here, right now. No one else—no counselor, no guru—can bring this peace to you. This is work each of us has to do on our own, learning from one another's stories.

Start with looking at the intention in your own home. What do you allow to take root there? Are there any skeletons that need to fall out of your closet? "This can be an invitation to face all the ghosts that have inhabited our physical, emotional, and spiritual residences," says psychotherapist Flor Fernandez.

How often have you invested in a life that looks perfect—with the perfect career, perfect clothes, a Pottery-Barn-perfect home—but at the same time fostered messy relationships with family, friends, co-workers, or neighbors?

Look at a typical day. What do you give your attention to, eat, purchase, relax with, visualize, attract, and act upon? What do you allow into your home? How do those things make everyone feel? How do they affect your relationships? Whom do you spend time with, form your opinions and make plans with? What or who guides you at your core?

What's supportive? What's destructive? Start being radically honest about your choices, knowing you can always choose more peaceful ones.

During the Iraq War, looters and soldiers pawed over the contents of the homes of Saddam Hussein and his sons. They found some deeply disturbing items, from pornography to drugs. But if we looked honestly at our own homes, what would we find? Americans are among the biggest distributors and consumers of pornography and drugs in the world.

It is easy to righteously lambaste Hussein for his brutality and human-rights injustices, which were in fact horrific. But now, as our own torture and abuse of Iraqi prisoners comes to light, we see that we, too, have invested in something ugly.

Committing ourselves to creating peace means we need to shine light on the ways in which we ourselves have been anything but peaceful in our lifestyles, consumerism, media, entertainment, relationships, and foreign affairs.

We produce more violence in movies and other media than any country on earth. We willingly let broadcasters pump an ongoing stream of murder, sex, mean-spirited characters, and other dark fare into our homes. We participate. We subscribe. We pay for this. We turn it on. We stay tuned.

We can invest in something greater. Setting the intention to be peacemakers means getting clear about who we are in the world and then cleaning house, literally and figuratively, as necessary. It means purging our own homes of whatever choices keep us from being peaceful people. An authentic housecleaning requires looking at everything we buy, embrace, and share with others, from our video games to our conversations. Do they raise the joy, love, and energy in our homes—and world—or drain them? What about our routines, schedules, food, visitors, hobbies, Web surfing, financial investments, weapons, and friends?

Of every choice you make, start asking yourself, "What is my intention with this? Does this increase the joy in my life, in our home, in the world?" If you find that it doesn't, make a new choice. Be creative. Be accountable. Be bold, and do what your heart tells you to do, even if others question your choice.

Author Maya Angelou says part of her personal housecleaning involves not letting prejudiced, harsh-minded people into her home because their ugly words cling to her drapes and seep into the walls and carpet.

"You are the window through which you must see the world," George Bernard Shaw said. Once we get our own homes in better order, we can start looking at our global home.

## • Question Your Government's Choices and Priorities

You are one. You are a powerful one. And to exercise your true power, you can't blindly accept what anyone tells you, no matter whom or what they represent. This is the time to get clear about your power and your intention. Constantly ask yourself questions about your focus, intention, purpose, and choices. Think and speak as a citizen of the world, as Martin Luther King Jr. urged, not just as a citizen of your own nation.

"Transfer your support to those working to eliminate violence, no matter where it is found or who is madly justifying it," says peace activist Colman McCarthy, who sows the seeds of peace through his Center for Teaching Peace.

McCarthy shares his inspiring messages with thousands of students, from elementary schools to universities. Question the questions, McCarthy says. Question why we have such extraordinary faith in violence but such extraordinary skepticism about nonviolence. Why do we teach our children so much about wars and warriors but not about peacemakers? Beyond tales of Martin Luther King Jr. and Gandhi, we teach them surprisingly little about those who have stood up and made a space for peace in the course of history.

In his many talks to students, McCarthy offers a 100-dollar bill to any student who can identify his list of 10 prominent peacemakers. He has yet to get a taker. Why is that?

These are the times to ask tough questions and follow where the answers lead us. Why is our nation more primed to declare war than others are? Why do so many people still believe war is our best option to resolve conflicts? Why? We can't progress as a nation unless we challenge the myths and misunderstandings that hold us back.

Assuming our power and setting new intentions in our lives demands honest, real reckoning. Our elected leaders have often chosen to arm terrorists and fuel already explosive situations. "We have allowed our government to bomb civilians, withhold medical supplies, and sell weapons to brutal thugs in every part of the globe," says author Barbara Kingsolver in *Small Wonders*.

We also have contributed to the poverty and despair that are the breeding grounds for terrorism. Our business and political practices have fueled the gulf between rich and poor. That gulf has never been wider.

"Today, an ordinary citizen of a poor, undemocratic, Muslim country, or a civil servant in a third-world country or in a former socialist republic struggling to make ends meet is aware of how insubstantial is his share of the world's wealth," says Turkish author Orhan Pamuk.

"He knows that he lives under conditions that are much harsher and more devastating than those of a Westerner and that he is condemned to a much shorter life," Pamuk says. "At the same time, however, he senses in a corner of his mind that his poverty is to some considerable degree the fault of his own folly and inadequacy or those of his father and grandfather. The Western world is scarcely aware of this overwhelming feeling of humiliation that is experienced by most of the world's population."

Do we realize what our investments have done to other people, how that may lead them to feel deep shame? Do we see that from that shame, they start to resent, even hate us? We can now set the intention to invest wisely, to make affirming choices, to ease the conditions that lead to inequities, and to listen deeply to our fellow human beings. We can intend to find common ground, not differences. We have a beautiful, unprecedented opportunity to be changemakers, to turn our lives in an entirely new direction. How very, very lucky are we. The possibilities are infinite. Dwell in those possibilities.

## • Celebrate Your Choosing Peace Instead of War

Celebrate those moments. We can catch ourselves a hundred times a day choosing resentment, bitterness, and righteous indignation or a sense of relief, a sense of inspiration, says author and teacher Pema Chodron. "Every day, we could think about the aggression in the world, in New York, Los Angeles, Halifax, Taiwan, Beirut, Kuwait, Somalia, Iraq, everywhere. All over the world, everybody always strikes out at the enemy, and the pain escalates forever. Every day, we could reflect on this and ask ourselves, 'Am I going to add to the aggression in the world?' Every day, at the moment when things get edgy, we can just ask ourselves, 'Am I going to practice peace, or am I going to war?'"

Pat yourself on the back each time you develop your stamina and strengthen your "muscles" of peacemaking. Reward yourself each time you successfully set the intention to anchor peace and are able to follow through. That is huge, especially while you are still somewhat afraid or unsure of yourself. "To stay with that shakiness—to stay with a broken heart, with a rumbling stomach, with the feeling of hopelessness and wanting to get revenge—that is the path of true awakening. Sticking with that uncertainty, getting the knack of relaxing in the midst of chaos, learning not to panic—that is the spiritual path," says Chodron in *When Things Fall Apart*.

Peace In Our Lifetime

# *Two*

# WORKING IT OUT

*I*t was a perfect summer afternoon when Bob Wicklund joined the fair that stretched along the banks of Portland's Willamette River. Mellowed by the music in the air, he rubbed shoulders with tens of thousands of other people. Like the strains of the music, all were blending in this peaceful moment—young and old, rich and poor, Anglos, Asians, blacks, the homeless, the disabled, urban and rural dwellers.

"Why can't my whole life be like this?" Wicklund wondered. "Or like that?" he thought, spying a sky-blue T-shirt offered by a vendor. On the shirt, a white dove floated in the words *Let There Be Peace on Earth, and Let It Begin with Me.*

"I wanted it," Wicklund said. "I wanted not just the shirt but the idea, the actuality of peace. Not just peace. I wanted to be rid of conflict—interpersonal conflict, mostly, but my internal conflict, as well. I hated it. I feared it.

"My environment seemed filled with unresolved conflicts. They took all my energy just to avoid them, to please the ones who were conflicting with me, to rescue those in need. The number of conflicts appeared to be building, getting out of control. My family, my job, my work, my community seemed filled with conflicts."

Everywhere he looked—conflict. In the Northwest, Wicklund saw environmentalists who wanted to save trees fighting fiercely with foresters who wanted to harvest them. In his home, his children were growing up and exploring life in ways that challenged his values. Wicklund hated all the conflict.

Who can't relate to his story? Our avoidance of conflict is universal. Most of us loathe conflict and try to avoid it at all costs. Maybe if we just sidestep our conflicts, we tell ourselves, life really can be one, continuous summer day at the fair.

Has that worked for you? Has it worked in our local, national and global disputes? Our inner peace and relationships usually just deteriorate further when we turn our backs on conflict and let disagreements fester.

To make peace in our personal worlds—and in the world at large—we need to wade into and become comfortable with conflict. We need to stop fearing conflict and learn to deal with it positively and purposefully, like any other challenge.

Each of us lives in various communities—churches, workplaces, offices, support groups—where conflict is inevitable. As long as human beings live and love together in clans, tribes, and nations and come together at potlucks and holiday gatherings, conflict will happen. It's normal. It's natural.

Whether you're hosting your family on Thanksgiving or conferencing with your staff, conflict pops up as surely as the crying baby in the middle of the movie or the neighbor who tries to convince you to vote the way he does.

Intensity will always percolate from a group of people with diverse ages, hurts, values, losses, beliefs, races, cultures, religions, and abilities. Community is precisely the place where the people you least want to be with show up, observes author Parker Palmer.

Let's face it: No matter how much we try to isolate ourselves, we can't avoid conflict. Even monks and nuns living a monastic life report having to work out their differences. When asked what the hardest thing was about leaving the secular world behind and

50

living a cloistered life in a monastery, one monk remarked, "The other monks."

Simply being human means being in conflict at times. So the trick is to become more confident and resourceful at handling conflict. Here are some ideas for easing the conflict in your life:

## Understand Why Conflict Makes You Squirm

Why do we retreat, simmer in silence, or avoid confrontation altogether? Could it be that many of us just never learned how to work out our differences with confidence?

To become more comfortable with conflict, take a look at how you've viewed conflict in the past. What were you taught about conflict in your family? How did you handle conflicts in your family, with your teachers, college roommates, your first boss, or during the first years of your marriage?

"The first educators in violence are our mothers and fathers. If they treat us with harsh language and physical violence we learn, 'Well, that's how I should solve my conflicts,'" says peace educator Colman McCarthy.

"If a child learns from adults at home that there's no way to deal with conflicts other than using fists, guns, or harsh language, the child will learn that."

Bob Wicklund says, "My childhood memories connected conflict to highly emotional states, to violence, to the possibility of death." Fortunately, he is now not only comfortable with conflict but helps schools and companies navigate theirs through his organization, Consensus Associates.

If Wicklund's early experiences with conflict are even somewhat similar to your own experiences, it's no wonder you run from conflicts. Why wouldn't you run away from danger as fast as you could? Or maybe you're one who pretends that everything is fine, just fine, knowing full well that land mines of resentment lie buried beneath the surface.

Lots of people go into marriages, jobs, and everyday life ignorant about how to resolve conflict well. Then they accumulate even more shame and regret each time their conflicts get out of hand, hurting others.

With all that discomfort, it's easy to assume falsely that our opinions, values, and behaviors will always cause such damaging conflicts, blocking us from healthy relationships. No wonder, thinking we have no other options, we rip into each other on the freeway, on the soccer field, and in our neighborhoods. We know no other way to get what we need.

Don't feel bad if you haven't scored top grades in Conflict Resolution 101. Many people, men especially, may still have scars from being toughened up for daily combat. David, now an inmate in Oregon, traces his "war consciousness" and lack of ability to deal with conflict to his childhood. "When I was six years old, I had an argument with a neighbor kid. My dad told me to fight the kid or that he would beat me to it within an inch of my life."

As David grew up, fighting with other boys was condoned by the old adage, "Boys will be boys."

Over the years, David continued to fight at times of conflict because of his fear of ridicule, fear of looking weak, and fear of not being a "man." He was told, "Real men are warriors; to survive you must be strong and ruthless. It was pounded into me that I had to always win no matter what it took, no matter what it cost."

## Consider Conflict in a Totally Different Way

Start to think about the possibility that conflict doesn't have to be scary. It can be healthy, even positive. Think of it as an opportunity for greater wisdom and growth.

Conflict serves a powerful purpose in our lives. It creates necessary tension, forces us to get clear about our values and needs, and allows us a chance to express those values and needs directly and honestly. It helps us become aware of our deepest desires and helps us be assertive enough to see that those desires are met.

Conflict helps us grow into the fullness of ourselves. As uncomfortable as it can feel, conflict helps us learn new, more loving ways of being with one another.

"Conflict is a call to creative problem solving," says peacemaker and author Louise Diamond. Having worked in war zones around the world, Diamond has seen how not dealing with conflict often drains people of their courage, power, and hope. When they run away from conflict, they channel that pent-up energy instead into crippling apathy, avoidance, or abuse of power.

Start, little by little, opportunity by opportunity, to become more comfortable with conflict. When a disagreement crops up at work or at home, visualize yourself staying confident and calm. See yourself staying cool and thoughtful as others speak their truth. Imagine yourself speaking your truth authentically and being heard and respected. Then, even if discussions become emotionally charged, you have already created an energy, an intention that the discussion will go to a peaceful place.

## Deepen Your Empathy for Others

Our neighborhoods are perfect material for this practice. Craig Cox, a contributing editor for *Utne Reader*, shared his experience of this in the January/February 2002 issue.

Cox and his wife, Sharon, then lived in a Midwest neighborhood where conflict broke out between some neighbors, Calvin and Geneva. The first time Cox heard gunfire at Calvin and Geneva's house down the block, he thought it was just "a one-time deal, the kind of random shoot-'em-up that at the time often punctuated midsummer evenings in our south Minneapolis neighborhood. I dutifully called 911 and filed the incident away in the back of my mind.

"After all, Calvin and Geneva had raised a family in that house, we'd been told. Their girls had played with the teenage girls who often babysat our kids. They came to our block parties and, though they clearly had their problems (Calvin had lost his job and was drinking too much; Geneva, too, hit the bottle), they'd been accepted as part of the neighborhood long before we arrived."

But when shots rang out again a few days later and then again a couple of days after that, the block went on high alert, Cox said. Sharon and Craig learned that the police were monitoring the developing feud between Geneva's nephews and the family across the street. "Meanwhile, out in the front yard, our two kids were showing their friends how to drop and roll if they heard shots."

The next Saturday afternoon, a car sped by and unloaded gunfire into Calvin and Geneva's front window. Not long after that, two young men, one armed with a shotgun, rushed from the house and drove away.

"The escalating level of violence down the block had now reached the point where Sharon and I were starting to worry about crossfire. We called a block meeting and were not surprised to find our tiny living room filled to the rafters. In the corner, Officer Steve Revor listened patiently as we vented our anger and frustration over the apparent crime spree at Calvin and Geneva's. One former neighbor tearfully revealed how constant drug dealing at the house had finally driven her family away from the neighborhood they loved. Someone else talked about condemning the house and forcing them out.

"We were, I recall, working up quite a froth of indignation when Officer Revor finally spoke up: 'Why don't we ask them what's going on?'

Silence.

'I'll just go down and get 'em, and we'll have a talk,' he said, smiling.

"The air left the room, and people who a moment ago were so clear in their resolve, so certain of the bad guys, gasped at the thought of confronting the enemy."

Soon a very sober Calvin and Geneva sat in front of the group and shared their story, Cox recalled. "We listened as Calvin, eyes downcast, told of how Geneva's nephews and their friends had gradually taken over the house and turned it into one of the city's busiest crack dealerships. He described how he'd been beaten up a couple of times in his attempts to evict these hoodlums from his home and how he wouldn't dare call the cops on them, for fear of his life. He'd been out of work now for a long time, he said, and felt useless, powerless.

"Geneva didn't say much. She seemed a little chagrined at having her home life displayed so openly to neighbors she'd known for so many years, but her attitude, if not quite contrite, was respectful. It seemed she felt some loyalty to her disruptive relatives and viewed the chaos as an unfortunate but unavoidable part of life in the big city. Her obvious embarrassment, her fear of judgment, the way she appeared slightly ticked off about the whole scene, combined to create, for me at least, a portrait of a real person. It was easy to see that Calvin was a victim in all this; Geneva's role was more complicated, yet no less human.

"None of us could any longer view this troubled couple as the enemy. Their very humanness disarmed the group, deflated our self-righteousness."

The gathering quickly turned into a forum to explore solutions, and many neighbors, including Craig and Sharon, pledged their support to Calvin and Geneva.

What happened in the neighborhood? Things quieted down for a while. Then a few weeks later, local police and FBI agents staged a raid on the house, and that ended the violence. Calvin and Geneva relocated, each to a different home.

Craig, Sharon, and their children outgrew their little bungalow and now live in another part of Minneapolis. "We're less concerned about gangs and guns now (crime has dropped all over the city in the past few years), but we're not so naive as to believe that the threat of violence and evil has disappeared from the world.

"It's still out there, but I'd like to think we're a little better able to confront and perhaps defuse it because of what we learned that afternoon with Calvin and Geneva, who changed in our minds from feared enemies into human beings after a half hour of hearing their stories."

An open, empathic heart can calm any conflict. It shows that even those we hate or fear are, at heart, people like us, struggling with challenges, vulnerabilities, choices, and usually the deep desire, like ours, for stable homes.

## Express Your Deepest Desire

Through our conflicts, we can tap into our real beliefs, values, and behaviors—and what we need most. Often, when peacemakers in military zones or combative organizations ask the parties involved not what they are fighting about but what they really, really need, peace breaks out. By sharing our feelings about the nature of a conflict, we can finally get to the root of it, and often the conflict dissipates.

Peter Forbes, president of the Trust for Public Land, has often seen this happen. TPL is a national, nonprofit organization dedicated to conserving land to improve the quality of life. Since 1972, TPL has helped protect more than 1.4 million acres in 45 states.

Many times, Forbes and his staff deal with willing land sellers, but other times, they have to walk through combative negotiations. Forbes has discovered that encouraging people to reveal what lies in their hearts often helps get to the heart of the conflict. This is what happened in the classic preservation of Walden Pond, the eastern Massachusetts site of Henry David Thoreau's famous home.

"This was the land that inspired Thoreau, who went on to inspire Gandhi, who went on to inspire Martin Luther King Jr. and many nonviolence and civil disobedience advocates," Forbes says.

In the early 1990s, as preservationists and others reeled in horror, land officials approved a large part of the Walden Pond area for two potential commercial developments. One was a 136-unit condo project. The other was a 400,000-square-foot office building. Many environmentalists, historians, teachers, and ordinary citizens were shocked at what they viewed as commercial exploitation of a treasured historic site.

This was a classic, polarized, land-use nightmare, which got uglier as the visibility of the controversy grew. "Musician Don Henley came and did concerts to raise awareness, and famous writers got involved. The developers, Phil Normandy and Mort Zuckerman, got up to 2,000 postcards a day telling them what assholes they were."

In the middle of this heat, Forbes set up a meeting with Zuckerman to try to negotiate an agreement to preserve the land. "I didn't know him from anything, and when I sat down, Zuckerman dumped a stack of hate mail out and said, 'What do you want to say to me?'"

"Luckily, the first thing that fell out of my mouth was, 'I really want to know what you love most about this land!' Zuckerman then paused and spent an hour telling me how he grew up next to Walden Pond. His grandfather was a state senator who tried to protect all of Walden Pond. He felt he was in that lineage, doing the best he could for it."

It turned out that Zuckerman's expressed love of the land and his emotions surrounding the property were "a much more successful starting place for that negotiation than hate mail. In very short order, less than three weeks, we were able to negotiate an agreement," Forbes says.

As this story illustrates, often the first step in any conflict resolution is just to listen. Listen to others voice their fears, their hopes, their worries about what might happen if the conflict escalates. Listen also to their dreams of what might be realized if the conflict were eased.

As others tell their stories, practice listening without judging, pressuring, scoffing, or intimidating—or eye-rolling, fingernail-picking or foot-tapping—to get others to cave in to your demands. This is a time to focus on raising hopes.

Often just having our dreams, fears, hopes, and worries heard is more than enough to help us remember what really matters and break long-standing tensions, finds Steve Schiola, a principal and former conflict-resolution administrator in the Poudre R-1 school district in Fort Collins, Colorado. "It puts a personal face on the conflict, which often has become abstract and blown out of proportion. Often, people have forgotten why they were arguing to begin with."

Whenever he gathered angry teachers and staff together and allowed them to share their truth, the tension usually ebbed. "I began with having them express their hopes for themselves and their school, if we could end the conflict. Then I would have them express their worst fears, if the conflict continued to escalate."

Just in sharing their deepest feelings, a palpable, powerful shift would occur, Schiola says. They would look around and see that the people they are in conflict with are usually caring human beings who, like them, just want a more peaceful school.

## Use Conflict to Find Your True Power

Have unresolved conflicts in your life ever caused you to lose hope or to use your power abusively? When we let conflict turn violent, we drain our power. Actively practicing conflict resolution, on the other hand, leads to true power. We feel potent when we see that we can stay calm and heart-centered and express our emotions clearly even if others become unbalanced, unfair, and combative.

You can learn how to master conflict and be a powerful mediator, tapping into your own power even in the middle of a conflict. Remind yourself that the frustration or anger you feel can be tapped into as a passionate, positive force. You can channel it for great, positive change. Tell yourself that it's OK to be passionate for positive good but not for blind revenge. The sense of outrage you feel about the situation you're facing can be a powerful tool for creating a better response, a better tomorrow.

This is the challenge for many schools now: to help children see that they can gain greater power by resolving their conflicts.

Try to express your emotions, including the fears that you've kept locked inside for too long. If you continue to keep them inside, they hold power over you. Once released, you take back your power to forge a new way, a more peaceful state.

Many schools nationwide are becoming amazingly expert at tapping the strong emotions that children often bring to school each day and using them for a positive good. Mike Mahoney, a school psychologist working at the Roseburg, Oregon, high school, has used mediation masterfully to calm potentially violent moments between students, many of whom had long resolved their conflicts with physical fights.

"I've seen mediation help these students gain insights and understanding into each other's behaviors. Then when they have a disagreement, they are more able to 'back off' and not approach each other in a provocative manner that would otherwise surely result in a fistfight. With greater understanding, they can more easily agree to disagree on certain issues."

Talking to the core of the issues is the key, Mahoney finds. "Once I had a very volatile situation with four students who started arguing in welding class. The fight involved two buddies against two buddies. A few of these boys were 6'5", 240 pounds and had a long history of fighting…When they first came to my office, I wasn't sure if they were going to blow or not."

But when Mahoney invited the boys to sit down and talk out their differences, it took only about 40 minutes to get to the root of their conflict, air it, brainstorm solutions, and create an agreement to stop fighting. The source of their conflict, which is so often the case in our own lives, wasn't at all what it appeared to be on the surface.

"It turned out that their fight erupted when one of the boys taunted another by saying, 'Your mom.' The boy had responded, 'I don't like you insulting my mother.'"

"What is it about that that offends you?" Mahoney asked the boy.

"I haven't seen my mother in so many years," the boy said. In fact, he didn't even know where she was. He still had the wound from her leaving.

All of a sudden, the boy who had thrown the "Your mom" insult got a somber look on his face. "It turned out that he was also from a dysfunctional family, and he'd felt abandoned by his father, who had never committed to his family and was a chronic drug and alcohol abuser."

In that moment of huge empathy, the boys were able to see the source of—and the similarity of—their pain. They saw themselves in each other, which can melt most conflicts.

"By talking over their feelings, the boys were able to see their differences in a whole different light. They were able to express feelings they weren't even aware of that they'd kept under the surface. They finally admitted they would really like to be friends."

Though their friendship never took off, the boys did respect each other and left each other alone for the remainder of their school years together. Most importantly, they learned there is a more positive way to resolve their conflicts. One of the boys stopped fighting at school entirely, graduated, and is now holding a job in his community.

"Like all of us, students are just looking to be respected, to feel they belong and are accepted and honored or loved. I believe mediation helps kids respect others, even if they don't agree with or get along with them. It teaches them how to be human, own their feelings, and deal with conflicts creatively and nonviolently."

Mahoney is so convinced of the power of mediation to ease differences and prevent violence that he helped document its effectiveness at his former school in New Jersey. "After our mediation program started, our discipline referrals and incidents of fighting dropped from 100 or so to six or seven a year. We were widely praised by the New Jersey school system."

## Talk Out Your Differences

As the following story shows, sometimes just the art of conversation can empower us and take us to higher ground. In the early stages of his distinguished career as a mediator, William Ury often saw how bottled-up emotions, once released, allowed people to go to a higher reality. He saw an extreme instance of this when he spent six months negotiating the peaceful settlement of a coal strike deep in Kentucky, in the heart of Appalachia.

"It was a bitter situation. They were packing guns, and there were bomb threats. I came in from Boston, and they thought I was from Mars.

"But during the six months we were there, I spent a lot of time inside the coal mine. And I taught the parties methods to talk about their differences rather than just walking out when there was a problem…And eventually, by and large, the miners learned how to handle their conflicts through negotiation."

Ury used the mediation experience with the coal miners as the basis of his thesis, "Talk Out or Walk Out."

Conflict will always be with us, says Ury, author of *The Third Side: Why We Fight and How We Can Stop* and other bestselling books on conflict resolution, but violent responses to it can end. "Violence is one option; talking is another, and people are gradually learning that they can probably realize their objectives more easily by talking than through violence."

Ury now works in other countries to try to stop civil wars before they break out. In Venezuela, where tensions are mounting and more people are arming themselves and fighting in the streets, talking about peace still holds great appeal and offers deep hope. Working on behalf of the Carter Center, Ury has found Venezuelans more than willing—actually eager—to talk out their differences.

"When we first went to Venezuela, we had a press conference with the message, 'There is no outsider who will rescue you. The outsiders can help and assist, but ultimately the answer comes from the Venezuelan people themselves.'"

The Carter Center gathered about 200 leaders from government, religion, academia, business, nonprofits, and communities. "This was a rare meeting because they usually don't get together and talk."

As part of the meeting, people divided into smaller groups. They explored ways to build bridges and prevent more violence. They wondered, for instance, if they could get the media to stop inflaming the conflict. So Ury and others met with members of the press. Finally, meetings were announced for the general public— pro-government and anti-government factions together—to try to talk out their differences. They had no idea how many people would be interested.

"We had 800 people show up. And out of that daylong meeting in a hot, stuffy theater, people stayed on. One woman journeyed 12 hours on a bus from some poor corner of Venezuela. She had just come from a meeting with some indigenous people, and they'd had a peace ceremony. She wanted to offer her prayer from that group. After the meeting, she immediately went back home on another 12-hour trip. There was a lot of energy and intensity in that meeting."

During the meeting, Ury asked if anyone was willing to be on a committee to sustain the dialogues for peace over time. He asked them to stay after the meeting. A passionate core of 70 people stayed.

"They promptly met three days later, and they've been meeting ever since. They call themselves Builders of Peace. They organize events, set out tables for dialogues on the streets, and invite people of different points of view to have conversations with one another. They've also reached out to the media to have new dialogues on radio shows to give people the sense that there is something larger happening."

In an increasingly manic world, it's easy to forget the simple art of talking out our conflicts. We forget that we have the ability to connect and heal through our conversations. We forget that we long to come together and dream of a brighter future. We forget that workable solutions can be found that honor all parties. We forget how to hold and respect each other's stories.

Let's remember. And let's also remember that most people around the planet have lived most of their lives in peace, not war. Let's remember that we can extend our peace to others. "Peace is the norm. It is time, then, to stop thinking of peaceful coexistence as merely a vision. It is a reality," Ury says.

## WHAT MORE CAN YOU DO?

- **Set Your Intention for Finding the Nonviolent Solution**

Commit to sowing and harvesting peace right where you are. Become a force for nonviolence. Join with that force already transforming the world as we know it. Nonviolence is "the most daring, creative, and courageous way of living, and it is the only hope for our world," says Mairead Corrigan Maguire, who earned the Nobel Peace Prize for her work in easing the conflict in Northern Ireland.

Ireland has been shining with greater peace. Ireland and its people wanted peace more than they wanted war. They wanted it so much they drew it to them with their will, their longings, their convictions—and their choices. They chose to learn how to live together in greater harmony.

At the grassroots level, Irish clerics, business people, politicians, neighbors, teachers, and family members mobilized and focused on how much more they wanted peace than fighting. They stood up for peace and learned how to resolve conflicts, offer forgiveness, find common ground, talk peacefully, and extend understanding, even in the midst of great tensions.

They chose peace. We can do the same.

## • Get Comfortable with Learning Something New

As with mastering any new skill, learning conflict resolution can take you to a new edge. You may feel anxious, scared, and uncomfortable—but you will feel that anyway if you run away from conflict. You may still feel awkward, but each time you deal with your conflicts in a healthy way, those uncomfortable feelings will lessen.

## • Take Responsibility for Your Own Behavior

Dealing with conflict with integrity means we have to look honestly at our own choices. Ask yourself whether you're typically the one who eases or inflames tensions. Look at any of your own cultural values and prejudices that may promote warlike behavior. Accept responsibility for choosing peace over violence, stability over destruction.

"What we don't understand, or refuse to accept, is that wars are the culmination of the violence we experience as individuals," says Arun Gandhi. "The world is like a confirmed chain-smoker who wants to cure his cancer without giving up cigarettes. We want to put an end to wars without giving up our violent intentions and violent relationships." Peace gets very personal.

- **Let Your Feelings Guide You**

The next time you're in conflict with someone, tune into how you feel and whether this feeling is accomplishing what you want. How do you feel about the person with whom you're fighting? Ask yourself if it feels good and is representative of what you want to give to the world. If you don't like the answers, think about a compromise or a new choice that feels more comfortable. Check in with your feelings to make sure your frustration with an individual is less about that person and more about the inequity or injustice at hand. Use those strong energies to heal what is broken.

# Peace In Our Lifetime

## *Three*

# ENDING OUR DEMONIZING

W hen the Gulf War was at its feverish peak, Unitarian minister Sarah Oelberg was attending a marathon meeting in New York City. After the meeting finally ended late one night, she headed to a favorite ice-cream shop to unwind.

She reached Amsterdam Avenue, where the crosswalk light was flashing, "Don't Walk." But she ran for it anyway. Oelberg only made it to the median before cars started to whip around her. A large, bearded, swarthy man dressed in Arab headgear and robes stepped onto the median from the other direction.

With the traffic rushing past them, Oelberg felt uncomfortable next to the man, so she tried to ignore him. "I've always felt safe in New York, but this man looked intense. His eyes sparkled with the passing lights."

He suddenly reached out, took hold of her shoulder, and turned her around to face him. "Have you ever seen a pigeon die? Well, I have," the Arab said.

Oelberg panicked. "I felt trapped. I envisioned my body being thrust under the wheels of the passing cars. I think I let out a little squeak. I was sure my luck had run out."

But then the man loosened his grip and, still looking deeply into Sarah's eyes, asked. "Have you ever seen a young boy die? Well, I have. Have you ever seen a soldier die? Well, I have."

Startled, Oelberg realized that the man was actually reciting a poem, a quite wonderful poem about death and war and peace and the consequences of killing. The Arab turned out to be a Muslim cleric, a man of peace sharing a haunting poem of protest about the Gulf War.

He'd just come from his own meeting with a group of American boys whose parents were in the army in the Gulf. He'd told the boys that Saddam Hussein was an extremist who wasn't following Islam, a religion of peace. Oelberg shared that her own son was in the war in Saudi Arabia, and she and the man had a deep, soulful discussion about conflict.

After Oelberg and the cleric parted, she realized she never got his name or a copy of the poem, if he even had one. Several years later, she saw a man on a subway platform who looked so much like her Arab friend from that December night that she rushed up to him, saying, "Have you ever seen a pigeon die? Well, I have."

This man peered at her strangely and walked away. "He probably thought I was crazy," Oelberg says. "I was apparently mistaken, but then, we know all Arab men with beards look alike, right?"

As we pause in the hectic medians of our own lives, with the intensity and force of life rushing past us, of whom are we suspicious? Whom do we stereotype? In the charged atmosphere since September 11, 2001, when Arab fanatics flew planes into the World Trade Center and the Pentagon, how many of us have adopted our own equivalent of the intense, wild-eyed Arab at Amsterdam Avenue, someone we fear and suspect will harm us, given half the chance?

Unless you're beautifully enlightened, you've likely targeted someone or a whole group of the Others whom you mistrust, maybe even hate. The Others are the "bad guys" who will lie, hurt, maim, cheat, and steal to get what they want, bringing you down in the process.

Demonizing makes even the most centered, well-intentioned people panic and find monsters in their midst, as Sarah Oelberg did that night in New York City.

When we start to see bogeymen everywhere, we resent people we don't even know. We turn against each other.

We each have our demons. Who are yours? Osama bin Laden? Your next-door neighbor? Muslims? Christians? George W. Bush? Corporations? Gay people? Working women? A former teacher? Your current employer?

The people we demonize are usually based on our own family conditioning, experiences, and prejudices. They're the perpetrators, the unjust, the hateful. They've made our life a holy hell. We never see our own role in the conflict.

These demons, we know, aren't even good, decent human beings but something subhuman. They scurry around and hide in caves, President Bush said repeatedly about Al Qaeda terrorists in 2002.

We, on the other hand, are the moral, wounded, preyed upon, blameless—oh, and lest we forget—the righteous victims. In every military campaign, we've tried to tell ourselves that we were the injured parties. We were the freedom lovers, and they were the evildoers.

Chris Hedges, a reporter for the *New York Times* who's covered atrocities in Sudan, Libya, Central America, and Bosnia, says in his book *War Is a Force That Gives Us Meaning* that we "demonize the enemy so that our opponent is no longer human. We view ourselves, our people, as the embodiment of absolute goodness. Our enemies invert our view of the world to justify their own cruelty....Each side reduces the other to objects—eventually in the form of corpses."

To guarantee that our demons stay far away from us, we layer on a heavy dose of moral superiority—or moral delusion—to say that God, the law, right, reason are exclusively on our side. How do we even begin to end our habit of demonizing?

# Recognize How Destructive Demonizing Is

Demonizing all the Others is one of the biggest roadblocks to peace. By the time we're hissing at and vilifying our so-called enemies, we've ditched all hope of ever finding common ground. We are thinking in black-and-white distortions, like assuming that anyone who speaks out against war is unpatriotic or that anyone for war is a murderer.

Our own wrong perceptions and our anger, fear, and hopes for revenge are the very grounds of more violence and terrorism, says Buddhist leader Thich Nhat Hanh. They're the seeds of more war, both within and without.

"Much violence, hatred, and despair are manifested now in America from our wrong perceptions of other people," Nhat Hanh says. "We have wrong perceptions about ourselves. We have wrong perceptions about others. On the foundations of all these wrong perceptions, we are afraid of one another. We hate each other. We want to destroy each other."

Recognize how demonizing diminishes your own power. "We rush to judgment about people who are different," says Oelberg. "We walk around with a wad of fear inside of us so we see potential assailants everywhere."

That kind of over-the-top fear freezes your compassion. It extinguishes your hope for a more loving world and dampens your desire to make a difference. How can our bellies be on fire with meaning and purpose when our hearts are paralyzed and paranoid?

Demonizing shuts down our innate impulse to love one another and come together in this too-conflicted world. "When we expect the worst of other people, we withhold the best of ourselves," Oelberg says.

How can each of us stop being so suspicious of others and disarm our internal "demonator"? How can we get beneath the surface of our judgments and better understand people different from us, based on their own merits? How do we focus on the goodness, not the darkness in others?

## Think About Why You Demonize

Stop hiding behind your fear of the Others. Take that fear out and examine it. Like getting to the root of any unwanted addiction, ask yourself what this habit's all about. What do you hope to gain by hating others so much?

Psychologists say we often regard the Others as evil because of our own insecurities and lack of perceived power. We don't feel safe or potent unless we keep ourselves fearful of and separate from them. We hope by ridiculing and hating others we will get some sense of comfort and superiority. By feeling better than someone else, we can banish our less-than feelings.

Is any of this true for you? Are you demonizing people in your life, or people you don't even know, because you want to feel safer or more secure? Do you ever enter into conflict to shore up your own sagging self-image or to fortify your own might? How much do our collective insecurities lead us to start wars? How often do our individual insecurities lead to fights with others around us?

Psychologists say we also demonize others when it gets too painful to look at our demons within—who doesn't have those?—and when it's too tough to examine our own shadows, our own addictions, abuses, or deceptions, we can see them all around us.

We want to believe that "the dark and the sinister are exclusively in the other, not in my own mind," says psychologist Susan Griffin. "One cannot realize that the awful other is also a part of oneself."

Does this represent your past at all? Children often don't dare speak of the family sins of alcoholism, incest, adultery, or mental illness. If any of these were taboo topics in your family, now as an adult you may righteously pounce on them in the Others.

What else leads us to blame and fear others? If someone has hurt you, it's only natural to fear they'll do so again. And the larger the pain and the deeper the secret, the more the demon looms. We try to stuff the pain away, but it's hard to keep a lid on it. So we squirm. We divert ourselves. We look at all those monsters "out there." We project our own darkness onto someone else.

## Look First at Your Own Demons

Does any of this strike a chord in your own life? How obsessed are you with making others wrong? How much time and energy do you invest in finding enemies around you? How eagerly do you jump on the soapbox and attack others? Look closely. Could any of your fears simply be projections of your own shadows? Do you loathe a particular trait you see in an ethnic or political group because you loathe that trait in yourself or someone you're close to? Do you attack that characteristic in another because you want to divert attention from yourself?

Examine the physical sensations you have when you think of a person or persons you loathe. What does it bring up in you?

If you want to start finding inner and outer peace, first sit with yourself. We can only start with ourselves. Sit quietly, and see what comes up. It may be uncomfortable to be still at first because our culture is so addicted to constant motion. But sit with the silence, and see what you discover.

Which demon in you is the fiercest? If you can honestly look at and recognize your own demons—your shames, regrets, times you hurt others, irresponsible behavior—you can more easily release them and start over. You can stop resisting your own shadows and stop projecting them onto others.

Our own demons usually don't look like Osama bin Laden but like addiction, depression, constant ridiculing, or crippling anxiety. They come in the form of misery, found Tom Heuerman.

Heuerman was really good at hunting down darkness all around him, so good he kept his own demons in the closet.

A special agent for the Secret Service during Richard Nixon's administration, Heuerman had gone into lots of shadowy places. He had investigated counterfeit cases, checked out forgeries, and protected both Nixon and Vice President Hubert Humphrey from bad guys.

But soon, Heuerman's own "bad guys" surfaced. "My inner life was in turmoil. I felt afraid, anxious, guilty, and angry. I went to a doctor, and he prescribed Valium—a quick fix. I thought a change in job and location would help me feel better—more quick fixes.

"I quit my job and moved my wife and two young daughters back to our home town. I was running away from myself, and I took myself with me."

Who can't relate to his story? How fast are you running these days? Do you often find yourself moving faster and faster when you really don't need to? How restless are you? Experiencing any insomnia, angst, overwhelming sadness? Any chance you might be running away from what you don't want to face?

Heuerman ran so hard and fast he eventually became an alcoholic. But with treatment, he brought his own angst to light and healed it. Now a life coach, Heuerman helps corporate leaders excavate their own and their organizations' shadows so they can be the most authentic, effective leaders possible.

Once our resistance to our demons is gone, they disappear, Pema Chodron says. She tells the story of Milarepa, a Tibetan hero who lived in caves and meditated for years. One day, he left his cave to get some firewood, and when he returned, his home was filled with demons. He knew they were just a projection of his mind, so he told them all about compassion and the oneness of life. All the demons left but one, the truly mean one. Like Milarepa, we all have that remaining demon we resist, the torment that just won't let go. Finally, after getting angry when the demon wouldn't leave, Milarepa surrendered even further. He walked over and put himself into the mouth of the demon and said, "Just eat me up if you want to." At that, the demon left.

## Examine Your Vulnerabilities and Shadows

Let's face it: One minute we're loving; the next, not so. None of us is perfect. Each of us is fully human. If we can integrate and accept all the parts of ourselves, even our shadows, then we can better make our peace with the humanity of others.

The truth is this: As human beings, we're rich, complex, and brimming with contradictions and mysteries. We're capable of immense love, which we want to magnify. But we're also capable of immense hatred. At times, we're the villains; at times, the victims. When we're tortured, we feel great pain. Sometimes that pain leads us to torture others, yet at other times, it gives us amazing empathy and compassion for others' suffering.

We can be achingly beautiful one minute and horribly ugly the next. We hide behind our shadows; we step out into the light with illuminating conviction. We are either light or darkness with each thought, moment, or choice.

In a sense, this is the story of mankind, says Tamuchin McCreless. "We are all surrounded by people who are much like us; they are almost like reflections. Sometimes we are afraid of them because we know they have the ability to hurt us as we know that we have the ability to hurt them. This drives some to want to destroy others before they are destroyed themselves. After all, befriending someone is sometimes more difficult than destroying them."

What a statement: Befriending someone is sometimes more difficult than destroying them. How often have we given up on peace too soon? How often have we found it easier to launch the first attack on our demons than to try for reconciliation? Where will it ever end? What if it ends with us? We can't go on this way. There is too much at stake. What if we stop reaching for our weapons of judgment and start to befriend those we fear?

When we can accept the fullness of our humanity, we can start to understand the humanity in others. We can stop righteously demonizing others for what we ourselves do. As we shine a light into our own murk, we can also find the seeds for our own regeneration that lie hidden with the drives and impulses that make us violent, says author Michael Nagler.

The awareness that each of us has faults "links us up to everyone on Earth, and that opens us up to courage and compassion," says poet and author Alice Walker.

Knowing that each of us is vulnerable and imperfect can allow us to feel great tenderness for one another. It makes us want to reach across what divides us to heal the separation.

It's only by developing compassion for those we once demonized that we'll be able to help them—and ourselves—heal and reach for something nobler. Only with such compassion can we choose to see not an evil person but a person who focused on hatefulness, as we all have. Only with a heart this open can we see no longer a demon but an individual who can now act from goodness and love, just as we can.

## Look at Your Wrong Perceptions

As Thich Nhat Hanh says, we often create terrorism from our own wrong perceptions of others. Examine whether your perceptions of your enemies are valid. What are they based on? Have you had actual experience with the people you are judging?

When Ronald Reagan was president, he repeatedly denounced the Soviet Union as the "evil empire." Soviet President Gorbachev was his enemy. Yet when Reagan finally got to know Gorbachev, he found the Soviet leader "pleasant, affable." The personal relationship they eventually developed helped soften the grip of communism in Russia and Eastern Europe. It also paved the way for the fall of the Berlin Wall and the Iron Curtain.

For 40 years, East and West Berliners were kept apart by the wall. But it finally came down, stone by stone, on November 9, 1989.

How often have you put up a wall so you could fear and demonize people, only to discover they were harmless, even likable, once you got to know them? Maybe they eventually became your friends. Think of someone you were recently suspicious of who proved to be innocuous. Even the worst demons can surprise us.

Before they even had a chance to meet, South African President P.W. Botha called Nelson Mandela a "communist terrorist," and Mandela called Botha "Crocodile." Once they finally met, each found a surprising number of things to admire in the other.

To Mandela's amazement, the first time they sat down to talk, Botha himself poured their tea. He treated Mandela with respect. Botha, likewise, was impressed by the depth of Mandela's knowledge.

Though tension still existed, they both agreed on the need for peace in South Africa. Mandela later said, "It was one of the most pleasant interviews I have had. He treated me with respect, very correctly. That is the image I have of him."

If demonizing dehumanizes us, one of the surest ways to reclaim our humanity is to meet our demons and discover their humanity. Get to know people on a personal and spiritual level so you no longer perceive them as separate from you. Hear their stories. Dig deeper. Go to "another dimension," says Thomas Merton. Go to the "genuine reality," or the "human dimension," as he called it. Whenever we fail to go to that human place, the Other too easily becomes an enemy.

Seasoned peacemaker and Mennonite professor John Paul Lederach remembers how he fell into this trap when he failed to see with his heart instead of his fears while working to end the civil war in Nicaragua. He was waiting at an airport on the Honduran border with Nicaragua. From afar, he saw a Honduran helicopter pilot dressed in fatigues and wraparound sunglasses. In Lederach's mind, the man was clearly a corrupt colonel, a symbol of the violent American and Honduran regimes devastating the peaceful Hondurans.

But when the evil colonel rose to meet an arriving plane, Lederach was stunned to see him greeting and assisting a handicapped 10-year-old girl limping along on crutches. The colonel clearly looked loving. "The colonel is a father, just like me," Lederach realized.

## Get to Know Your Demons

There is no better way to dispel our demons than to befriend them, or at least to get to know them on a deeper level so we won't see them as Other ever again. This is what Julie Goschalk has done, inspiring others to do the same.

Before World War II, there were more than 250 people in Julie Goschalk's father's family. After the Nazis' genocide of the Jews, only her father and 10 family members were left alive. Her mother's parents were killed at Auschwitz.

But Goschalk said her parents never talked about their losses or the Holocaust. Like many Jewish families, they stayed silent, hoping they could forget and spare their children the pain of knowing.

Still, Goschalk always knew something horrible lived in her home, even if it wasn't spoken of. Shadows that don't get held to the light grow and magnify. We also tend to get stuck in our roles as victims—or as abusers.

Goschalk learned this when she finally met her first German person—a fellow college student. She was so terrified, she immediately reverted to being a victim, even though she herself hadn't even been born until after World War II. "I was sure he would look at me and say, 'Hitler should have made soap out of you, after all.'" But when Goschalk finally met the German man, no such thing happened. They had a warm conversation.

In 1987, Goschalk, by then a Boston social worker, broke her own silence about the Holocaust. She began to seek out and listen to conversations that had been repressed for too long. In the Boston area, she helped facilitate a German/Jewish dialogue group between the children of Jewish Holocaust survivors and the children of Nazis.

How did she face her fears of Germans and find the courage to sit with such raw stories and memories about this hidden subject? How can you face your fear, sit face to face with your dire enemy, and listen to what they have to say?

Goschalk remembers feeling "incredibly nerve-wracked," her heart pounding furiously.

But she also remembers that she was curious, and that curiosity about the Others allowed her to overcome her fear. "I was curious enough to see what they were doing with their history. Would they acknowledge it? Would they be defensive? I had a certain curiosity to see how they coped with it. I know my nightmares and my depths of sadness, these wells of sadness. I wanted to know if they had any of this.

"I really think what brought us together was not some grand measure of healing or forgiveness but to see whether we had anything to say to each other," Goschalk says.

The German/Jewish dialogue group's mission deepened in 1992 when they were invited by an Israeli professor, Dan Bar-On, to attend a first-time meeting between sons and daughters of Nazis and children of Holocaust survivors. But this time, the meeting was to take place in Germany.

Meeting in Boston was one thing, going to Germany entirely different, Goschalk remembers. She was panic-stricken at the idea. She wrote how inconceivable the whole experience seemed at the outset in a *Boston Globe* article, "The Holocaust Facing the Enemy."

"After all, these were the descendants of the people who had tried to murder my parents and who had indeed killed the majority of my family."

But once again, she let her curiosity, not her panic, lead. How did they cope, she wondered? How did they deal with their family history and continue to live in their communities? She had many other questions.

The minute the meetings began on German soil, Goschalk saw that the people she met face to face and heart to heart were human beings who, like her, had suffered horrific losses. Many were still horribly ashamed and guilt-ridden, even emotionally crippled by their fathers' actions.

Many had deep sadness and remorse but, because their relatives had been Nazis, didn't feel entitled to share their feelings. They were emotionally stunted, believing they should suffer forever for their fathers' crimes against humanity.

One German woman said that her mother kept telling her, when she was a little girl, that her father was missing in the war. So she was always waiting for her dashing daddy to come home. But at some point in her adolescence, someone slipped and told the young woman that her father was dead.

Her father, it turned out, had been a Nazi SS general and was executed for crimes against humanity in 1946. Handsome daddy was actually a horrific murderer. She was his illegitimate daughter. In her 30s, this woman eventually found a photograph of her father and, even more shocking, actual footage from his trial.

Hearing such stories of suffering, Goschalk found the answers she'd been looking for her entire life. She discovered she was capable of deep empathy and compassion. She realized how much she shared with her former enemies. "As soon as we Jewish survivors started to talk about our experiences growing up with our parents....the Germans would just crumble. They were so distraught, guilty, and shame-filled, and I was actually bothered by that. They didn't do anything. They weren't murderers. They had just been children. Their grief and shame just blew me away. There was such a connection between us at that moment."

Goschalk came to see that "we were all on the same side. We looked at the events of the past in the same way and were trying to do something about them. We were trying to connect, educate ourselves and, in a way, be peacebuilders."

When it came time for Goschalk and the group to disband and go home, they found themselves "behaving like a large family who had not been together for many years and could not bear to part. Photographs were taken and addresses exchanged. People were hugging and thanking each other, and then we all went our separate ways."

Goschalk said the meetings were like a cleansing. "I felt kind of light afterward. I really felt euphoric, like my feet were not touching the ground. I was energized and absolutely awed at what had taken place."

The awe and wonder continued. After the meeting, Goschalk and a friend, scheduled for a return flight the next morning, were discussing where to spend the night. An unlikely option presented itself.

The German woman who had discovered she was the illegitimate daughter of the Nazi SS general offered them her home. Not only did Goschalk accept the invitation, but all three women stayed up late, sharing even more stories. Goschalk and the German woman are now close friends.

"If someone had suggested to me even six months ago that I would be spending the night at the German home of a Nazi SS general, I would have declared such a proposition preposterous," Goschalk wrote in the *Boston Globe* article.

But she got to know the "other dimension" of that woman. With deep affection in her voice, Goschalk says the woman she once viewed as the Other is an "incredibly sensitive, thoughtful, genuinely kind human being....As a human being, she is wonderful."

# Accept That We Each Hold a Piece of the Truth

An extremely powerful way to disarm our enemy mindset is to accept that each of us holds a piece of the truth, says Arun Gandhi. As India struggled for independence from the British, his grandfather wouldn't even allow supporters of his nonviolence movement to refer to the British as "the enemy," even when the conflict escalated and grew ugly. At the height of the tension, Gandhi organized the now-famous "salt marches" to the sea as an act of civil disobedience. The marches attracted thousands of people, who were often beaten with clubs by the police as they walked, recalls Arun.

"My grandfather always said, 'They are our friends, and we are trying to transform their ways.' He showed me that when we have an enemy mindset, the next logical step is to think evil of others, and that opens the door to negative thoughts and ultimately violence."

The moment we can finally accept our true nature and that of everyone around us, we are suddenly more liberated because we can reach one, powerful conclusion. It is a conclusion that, if truly lived by each one of us, would instantly make the world more peaceful: We can be responsible only for our own beliefs and choices. Only I can choose what my life will represent. Then when I am hateful, I can stop, make amends, start over, and choose to be more loving.

I can heal only my own demons and take responsibility for my choices, but I can't do so for you. I can live from my own values, but I can't demonize you into embracing them, too. I no longer have to beat you up and make you wrong to make my truth right. I no longer have to make you believe in my God, my leader, my favorite food, my religion, my, my, my, my whatever. How liberating is that?

If we can reach this state of acceptance, we no longer have to face off with our enemies. We no longer need to call for revenge and can instead feel compelled to call for greater peace. We can treat others with more respect and kindness in our offices, grocery stores, schools, streets, and homes, and in doing so, raise our own energy to a higher place, inspiring—not shaming—others into raising theirs.

We can become larger versions of ourselves. We can become powerful peacemakers able to calm conflicts before wars erupt, knowing that conflict is found in all our human hearts—conflicts that, unresolved, will keep us armed to the teeth, lurking in shadows, fearing and stalking one another when we should be caring for each other. "The cause of war is our collective failure to recognize that humanity is one family," says Eric Wenzel.

## Get to Know Real People

"I wonder what would happen if we responded to the real people in the real places where we live instead of to the stories we have heard about what has happened to other people somewhere else," asks Sarah Oelberg, the minister who once feared the "intense, wild-eyed Arab."

Have real experiences with real people. Deliberately cut through political lines and barriers and see how these are largely fabrications. Find out how similar, not separate, you really are. Find out what makes your demon a person just like you.

Seeking Common Ground is a program in the Rocky Mountains that allows Palestinian and Israeli girls to see the genuine in each other. Director Melodye Feldman remembers how difficult it was to get the girls to do this the first summer they came together.

"The minute they arrived, we took away their identification and passports. This wasn't to keep them here but to allow them to see one another not as Palestinians or Israelis but as people. They could now say whatever they wanted without their families or governments looking over their shoulders," Feldman says.

But the girls' anger and fear was intense. "The first time they were in a room together, they yelled and screamed at one another until many were hoarse. They came to us and said, 'We just can't do this anymore.' So we said, 'Would you like to learn another way?'"

The girls were guided to sit and listen to one another respectfully, with open hearts. But the most miraculous sense of seeing the genuine came in the evening, Feldman says. "It was like divine intervention. The girls were supposed to divide up, Israelis with Palestinians, and sleep together in tents. But they still didn't want to sleep with their enemy. But all of a sudden, there at 11,000 feet, it started to storm with lightning strikes. The girls had no choice but to dive into their tents."

The next morning, an Israeli girl came running out of her tent yelling, "It was like a miracle. They will never believe this back home. When I woke up, I was curled up with the head of a Palestinian girl on my shoulder and, snuggling next to her, lying on her shoulder, was the head of an Israeli girl."

From then on, the girls could no longer restrain their innate curiosity about the Other or their keen desire to connect. They soon were listening to one another's heartbeats, feeling each other's pulses, looking into one another's eyes, and discovering the preciousness of one another.

We can all do this work together, as those girls do. If we can help one another bring our demons to light, we take away their power to hurt us anymore. The darkness is totally extinguished by that intense, loving light. If we can help one another banish our shadows, we can surely help one another bring forth our light.

## Listen to the Stories No One Wants to Hear

Sometimes we need to sit with and hear some truths, no matter how horrific or painful, to banish our demons. This truth-telling promoted the healing of both the perpetrators and victims of apartheid's long reign in South Africa. Archbishop Tutu knew that, if reconciliation were ever to occur, it was crucial to uncover the full truth of what had happened, no matter how brutal. "Our slogan was 'The truth hurts, but silence kills,'" he says.

Tutu set up the Truth and Reconciliation Commission for people to come to and tell their stories. Initially, he was afraid people wouldn't be willing to talk. But the commission ended up gathering more than 20,000 statements.

"People had been bottled up for so long that, when the chance came for them to tell their stories, the floodgates opened. I never ceased to marvel, after these people had told their nightmarish tales, that they looked so ordinary. They laughed; they conversed; they went about their daily lives looking to all the world to be a normal, whole person with not a single concern in the world," Tutu says.

"And then you heard their stories and wondered how they had survived for so long carrying such a heavy burden of grief and anguish so quietly, so unobtrusively, with dignity and simplicity."

At Search for Common Ground, Susan Collin Marks works with people from all sides of any conflict in Africa, the Middle East, the Balkans, Indonesia, and the United States. SCG is not an advocate for any one side but for the process of finding a nonviolent solution to conflict, for reconciliation, and for helping build sustainable systems out of the ashes of war.

This means that Marks engages with people others condemn as evil or bad. Her personal way of dealing with this is to see them not as demons but as human beings who, like all of us, have both light and dark aspects.

Marks tells the story of facilitating a meeting in Washington, D.C., at which rebel and government leaders from an African country met in a neutral setting to talk about their differences. Much violence and bloodshed had been spilled in their country.

Several months after the meeting, Marks happened to visit that part of Africa, and though she had nothing formal set up, something told her to try to meet with one of the rebel leaders, a man responsible for many, many deaths.

"To my surprise, his office agrees that I can meet him. People are milling around with AK-47s. Many 'big men' of Africa are there to pay court to this African leader. They eye me, I suspect, because I am the only woman not serving tea, and I am the only white person."

Much to his aides' displeasure, the leader waved them aside and invited Marks into his room, alone. "I am mystified....But when we meet, this leader immediately says to me, 'I trust you. I trust you because of the way you handled that meeting in Washington, D.C. You were fair to everyone.'"

In that moment, Marks was able to see that how we choose to live each moment shapes the flow of our lives. A meeting thousands of miles and many months away, conducted with respect and compassion for all sides caught in the horrors of bloody conflict and with the intention of creating some connection between them, had generated this opportunity to talk quietly in an atmosphere of trust with an influential leader in the heart of Africa. It is a living example of how anyone and any reality can change at any time. It all depends on our choices.

The rebel leader then asked Marks, "Why are you here?"

"It seems to me," Marks said, "that it must be very difficult to honor the man as well as the general in you." She remembered that she was saying this to a man who had on his hands the blood of thousands of people.

How did the brutal demon respond? "He starts to weep and says, 'Yes, yes. It is so hard for me to reconcile the man and what I am doing here,'" Marks remembers.

Marks and the leader talked further, and she sensed an opening. "I can't speak to you of whether you should or shouldn't be in this war. All I can do is remind you that as a general and as a man, you hold in your hands the future and lives of the millions of people who live in your country. When you go forward and make military decisions, try to remember that. You personally hold millions of human beings in your hands," Marks said, cupping her hands.

Marks met with the African leader again twice. He told her how calming it had been for him to be seen in that way. As in many pivotal moments in peacemaking, Marks can't predict the impact of that encounter. But what she does know is that we all are interconnected; we all have the opportunity to heal ourselves and each other in every moment; and we can all draw on our courage and compassion to reach out to others, even so-called enemies.

Speaking from our hearts is liberating beyond words. It allows us to see the spirit within each of us. It allows us to look into one another's eyes and see our very souls. We can end this feeding frenzy of "demon" and "victim" when we recognize that we belong to one another—and we all want the same things. We want security, safety, love, and acceptance. Our deepest longings and our deepest fears are identical. In this recognition, common ground is discovered that has no room for isolation, separation, and hate.

# WHAT MORE CAN YOU DO?

- ## Change Your Mind About Your Demons

At any point, you can choose to change your mind. You can let go of the judgment you have of someone and embrace an entirely new truth. Growing up in a Jewish American family in the 1940s and 1950s, peacemaker Louise Diamond grew up aligned with the state of Israel, cheering for its victories, grieving for its losses. In her book *The Courage for Peace*, Diamond tells how she was conditioned to view the Palestinian world as enemy territory. The Arabs hated all Jews and only wished for their extinction, she believed.

When she was in her 40s, Louise Diamond had her own liberating experience from her shadow beliefs. "I was sitting in the home of a Palestinian family during the Intifada, experiencing with them the hardship of living under Israeli military occupation. As gracious and generous as the family was, I still felt uneasy.

"Then my host expressed a most astounding thought. 'We don't hate the Jews,' he said. 'We don't want to push them into the sea. We only want to live side by side with them, in peace and respect.'"

Diamond said her internal voice immediately shouted, "'Oh yeah? What a lie! I don't believe that for a minute!' Having heard the opposite about Palestinians for forty years, there was no way I could credit any truth to that statement."

But over the next few days, she continued to hear more Palestinian people express the same hopes and feelings. "Each time, I could feel the words bounce off the hard knot in my mind and heart that had been trained to believe that all Arabs hated all Jews and, like many nations throughout history, wished for our extinction."

Gradually, she began to ask herself if it could possibly be true. Could most Palestinians really want to live peacefully with Israelis, as neighbors?

"Slowly, slowly, over time, I allowed the witness of my eyes and of my direct experience of these wonderful people to soften that hard knot. As it dissolved, so did the image of the enemy I had carried all my life. In its stead grew a clear, more realistic picture of fellow human beings, just like 'us'; living with fear and pain, just like 'us'; caught in a violent cycle of action and reaction, just like 'us.'"

## • Go Within

Be willing to sit with and get to know your own demons. What haunts you still and begs to be healed? Free yourself. Strike a match in the darkness and see what's sitting there. Often, much to our surprise, we see that all along we've been hiding our own shadows, as well as our light. We're denying the fullness of all that life is, challenges and all.

- **Accept Your Humanity**

Isn't it true that, while you love your children, at times you do things, consciously or unconsciously, that hurt them? Isn't it true that, on any given day, you may lie, steal, or evade the truth, yet in another moment, be generous, honest, and full of integrity? "One might wish that reality was such that there would exist bad people who sneakily do their wrong deeds, and we only had to isolate and destroy them," said Russian author Alexander Solzhenitsyn. "The limits between the good and the bad, however, go right across any human heart."

- **Monitor Your Daily Demonizing**

Begin to notice your demonizing patterns. Realize that you create your demons. When you fixate on the darkness in others, you give it more power. You magnify it. What we pay attention to expands. Try to get more conscious of your demonizing patterns. Look at your own, immediate world, from your office to your neighborhood. Whom do you fear and avoid? Whom do you judge as evil? Is there someone with a different cultural background, religion, political affiliation, or life philosophy who mystifies, scares, or angers you?

We are especially wary when the Others come from a culture, clan, or group of people we associate with past harm or danger.

Spot the times you make yourself the judge and convict others "guilty as charged." Even if you feel your actions are pure, take a closer look at your thoughts and words. This is a subtler way we demonize. Look at just the last 24 hours.

Maybe you were driving to work this morning, and a driver cut you off, so you yelled, "You dumb jackass!" While you were shopping last night, you overheard a mother yelling at her child at the mall, so you sniffed, "Abusive mother." To better curb the habit, get more conscious of how and when you demonize.

- ## See the Mirrors Everywhere

As you start to look at your own demonizing patterns, ask yourself: Have I ever done the things I now harshly judge her/him for? Have I ever tongue-lashed my child while shopping? Have I ever cut other drivers off? Are they mirrors of me?

Parenting is always a humbling mirror to hold up, says Pema Chodron. She used to feel outrage when she read about parents abusing their children. "I used to get righteously indignant—until I became a mother. I remember very clearly one day, when my six-month-old son was screaming and crying and covered in oatmeal, and my two-and-a-half-year-old daughter was pulling on me and knocking things off the table, thinking, 'I understand why all those mothers hurt their children.'

"I understand perfectly. It's only that I've been brought up in a culture that doesn't encourage me that way, so I'm not going to do it. But at this moment, everything in me wants to eradicate completely these two, sweet, little children."

Continue to watch how you misjudge others, even in routine ways. As a daily peacemaking tool, Colman McCarthy empathizes with other drivers. Instead of tailgating drivers who cut him off in traffic, he calmly lets them pass and tells himself, "Oh, yeah, I've done that, too."

Try to hold yourself to this practice for a week. When you start to condemn someone, ask yourself, "Have I been in that exact spot before?" This practice can take all the sting and separateness out of our interactions.

We're all fully and gloriously human. And knowing we are so much alike in our humanness, shortcomings and all, is a great opportunity to feel more expansive, generous, and connected to others.

We all have beauty within. We all have anger and violence within. Even Jesus, Gandhi, and Buddha had these beasts inside them. Nelson Mandela and Mother Teresa also knew anger, jealously, and loneliness, Pema Chodron says. "They're people who made friends with themselves and therefore made friends with the world. They're people who developed the bravery to be able to relate to the shaky, tender, fearful feelings in their own hearts and therefore are no longer afraid of those feelings when they're triggered by the outside world."

Acknowledging our own vulnerabilities doesn't mean we heap more humiliation on ourselves. It's about developing the courage and compassion to sit with ourselves and see that we carry the potential for both goodness and destruction. Dual forces exist within us, and we can choose to feed what is noble and fine.

## • Continue Your Own Personal Reckoning

Knowing that life is a mirror and that we attract more of what we invest in, why are you still investing in what no longer serves you? What secrets do you still need to uncover to be truthful and authentic? Where do you need to withdraw your support of violence? If we're intent on creating a more peaceful world, we have to have a conversation with ourselves about the times we also have acted without spiritual integrity and fueled violence.

If we're passionate about bringing the shadows of terrorists and others to light, we also have to illuminate our own shadows that keep peace from shining in our lives. We have to own our choices. We have to be responsible for the times we armed ourselves with weapons of mass destruction, whether loaded words or abusive actions. What bombs have you detonated by shattering relationships, trust, or commitments? We have each been oppressor and oppressed; we've each committed many "subtle killings" that, unless brought to the surface and aired, will continue to keep us at war within.

All of us, says author Lama Surya Das, have "internal rap sheets to remind us of times we failed to be sensitive, that we failed to love and cherish all life. Acknowledging our transgressions, repenting, and vowing never to do it again is a way of healing our karma and healing ourselves. It turns us around and redirects us on a finer, more noble course."

These are the times to stop hiding in our shadows and to bring them and ourselves to a new light. These are the times to take full responsibility for our failings and release ourselves from the shame we've been carrying. Only then can we truly have the gift of inner peace and radiate that peace to the world.

## • Does This Feel Good?

Another way to become conscious of and transform your demonizing: Check in with your feelings when you demonize. How does it impact your inner peace? In the vein of Dr. Phil, ask yourself, "How's that working for you?"

Does judging the Other make you feel better or make you feel angrier, more paranoid and fearful? Does it make you squirm, remembering something similar that you did in the past?

Identifying your own pattern of demonizing isn't about wearing a hair shirt of shame and guilt. You don't want to heap on any more remorse and skitter farther into the shadows. You want to shine a light on the full truth of your being. You want to see clearly, without any excuses or lame justifications, the truth that we all fall down at times; the truth that we are more alike than we are different; the truth that we are deeply connected with one another. And when we choose to magnify the best, most loving aspects of ourselves, we all benefit greatly.

## • See Flawed Organizations as Human

Peace, then, can be our collective willingness to recognize that we all are part of one, global family, and if the family can stop attacking itself, it can begin to shore up its connections. We human beings can stop pointing fingers at the Others and start extending more support and understanding to those we have ostracized.

What a lighter reality that would be. What an opportunity to burn with the desire to reconcile with others, not harm them. Our passion can be about using our fire to transform and correct situations, not to send them up in flames.

When we develop our awareness in this way, it is much easier to see others with more tolerant eyes. We begin immediately to seek to understand, not condemn or polarize. It's easier to look at our collective, cultural shadows and see that, of course, all our institutions, from the military to churches, would have shadows, because those organizations are made of up people, just like you and me, who are both darkness and light.

With more awakened eyes, we can start to see that, naturally, corporations, political groups, even the Cub Scouts, Girl Scouts, and Disney World have their own shadows. That's because the people within them are human, capable of both harming and helping. They are full of people just like us, processing, growing, still working on their own consciousness.

Kenny Moore, a corporate executive and former monastic, knows well the imperfections and shadows of organizations. "All organizations, religious as well as secular, are fallible institutions made up of frail human beings. Never perfect. Often honest. Occasionally flawed and greedy. It's in all of us," says Moore.

Moore spent 15 years in a monastic community. Now he's the corporate ombudsman and human-resources director at KeySpan Energy. The only difference between the two types of organizations? "The latter pays better," Moore jokes. In both organizations, Moore found that the vast majority of people are good and often doing their best in a flawed, human system.

But "when the proverbial dung hits the fan, we rush to judge and condemn. Especially those in authority. What goes unexamined is the deeper question: What's my contribution to the problem? The degree to which we believe we are outside the problem is the degree to which we fuel it. If spirit is everything, we are part of everything."

## • Find Common Ground

As you get to know the genuine in others, try to find some common, shared experience to form a bridge on which to connect. Ask them about their pain, losses, triumphs, and joys. Find out who they really are. Eventually, Julie Goschalk's reconciliation allowed her to go full circle and see how much alike we all are. She was able to see firsthand the idea that we are all things, from darkness to light, capable of both immense love and intense hate.

In 1997, she joined a dialogue with black and white South Africans, Catholics and Protestants from Northern Ireland, and Israelis and Palestinians. She had wanted to join the South African discussion group but soon realized that was because she was too scared to be in the Palestinian/Israeli group, so she joined the latter. She and others told their stories, and by the time the Palestinians began to speak, Goschalk began to squirm.

"Again, there were tales of persecution, fear, loss, and unbearable humiliation. I couldn't believe what I was hearing. How was this possible? The more I heard, the more I cringed. I felt embarrassed to be Jewish. I could not bear the thought that my fellow Jews were inflicting such pain and horror on these people. I felt exhausted and did not want to be there."

Being suddenly thrown into the perpetrator role was extremely hard, she added. "It felt crummy. It was like putting the shoe on the other foot."

But the more others shared their stories over the next four days—Jews, Palestinians, Irish, South Africans—the more learning, empathy, and healing took place. "Obviously this was only a tiny beginning, but if in only four days we were able to begin to build a bridge across an apparently impossible gap, I feel there is hope for others to do the same."

Peace In Our Lifetime

## *Four*

# CHANNELING ANGER & FEAR

*A*nger breeds anger. That seems to be the wake-up call of our times. The more ugly offensives we launch, either militarily or in our personal affairs, the more shell-shocked we are when uglier waves of violence hit us in return. The CIA calls this "blow-back." Legions of us are blow-back-weary folks.

We're tired of being bludgeoned and berated by our own personal fights and the fights on the news each day. "We are becoming maladaptive as a species because we fight too much. We are poised to remove ourselves from the face of the earth because we can't stop fighting," says Marianne Williamson.

At this point in our evolution as human beings, with such immense richness of people and cultures, religions and nationalities, beliefs and dreams, we should be brimming over with blessings. These should be the glory days. We should be turning up the lights, celebrating our unique gifts, and filling our global home with our songs of joy.

But instead, too often, we're casting shadows, cursing our differences, and burning the house down. But this is the time for a different kind of global bonfire. This is the time to light a new, brighter fire to extinguish the flames of hatred. Rising numbers of people are blazing with hopeful ideals, not hopeless infernos.

This is the time to spread peace, because the flames of violence are rapidly burning back on themselves, desperately trying to gain a foothold on already scorched ground. We see this daily with the deaths, destruction, looting, and raging mobs in the Middle East, Africa, and other hot spots in the world. How do you and I create the kind of fiery soul force that Gandhi described, Martin Luther King Jr. kindled, and Jesus, Buddha, and so many others have modeled?

We keep transforming our anger to purpose and passion. We keep lighting the fires of kindness and compassion. Once you understand how and why your anger arises, start to have critical conversations with yourself, as King did, to understand and calm your anger. King often talked to himself for guidance, saying, "You must not harbor anger. You must be willing to suffer the anger of the opponent and yet not return anger. You must not become bitter. No matter how emotional your opponents are, you must be calm."

Begin to talk with yourself about your vision and desire for your anger. Consider using your anger not to get your way but to help humanity find its way again. Think of channeling your anger for the highest good.

Instead of responding to every provocation or perceived threat with violence, isn't another way possible? *Why do we think that killing those who kill to show that killing is wrong is a good idea?* I read on a bumper sticker recently. Can't we lift up our souls with a different message, a new response, and transform the pain of anger into the pleasure of joy?

Respond to darkness by retaliating with light, suggests Laura Blumfeld, author of *Revenge: A Story of Hope.* "Revenge doesn't have to be about getting back. It can be about getting better. You can get over that feeling of powerlessness by building yourself up and strengthening American society, whether that means volunteering at your local church, or organizing your community to build a new playground, or teaching literacy. Retaliate with light."

Meeting anger by retaliating with light? What a magnificent idea. Could it work? Could we give it a try? How do we begin? "When anger arises in the mind, when fear becomes present, it can either make life hell or reveal another opportunity to enter heaven," Steven Levine says.

What if we let our anger reveal heavenly opportunities for something greater for our lives? This is how we can use our anger for the highest good, here and now. Under the brutal apartheid regime of South Africa, Nelson Mandela was imprisoned for 27 years. If anyone had a right to be angry and bitter, Mandela did. But he saw his imprisonment as an opportunity not to harden his anger but to soften the hearts of his white wardens. He wisely viewed his guards as "necessary allies in the struggle" to end apartheid.

"Hostility was self-defeating," Mandela said. "There was no point in having a permanent enemy among the wardens." He also wanted his fellow South Africans to see that "I loved even my enemies while I hated the system that turns us against one another."

In prison, Mandela learned how to "live together, to transcend our prejudices, to resolve our differences amicably, to respect one another, and together to reach towards cooperation and attainable common goals."

Mandela said, "I came out mature."

How do we use our anger to reach greater maturity?

## Decide What Kind of Person You Want to Be

Like Mandela, we have to decide what to do with our anger. By now, many of us have heard the story of the Native American grandfather who told his grandson, "I feel as if I have two wolves fighting in my heart. One wolf is the vengeful, angry, violent one. The other wolf is the loving, compassionate one."

The grandson thought about this and asked, "Which wolf will win the fight in your heart?"

And the grandfather answered, "The one I feed."

Which wolf do you want to feed in yourself? It doesn't work to blame the violent culture, the angry people around us. We aren't victims. We have a choice. This is an inside job, extended outward.

Which are you motivated to feed and focus on—the snarling, angry, vicious, fearful wolf or the loving, compassionate, accepting one?

## Look at Your Anger History

It helps to look back on our choices about anger, both individually and as a society. How much energy have you invested over the years in keeping anger alive? Anger at your partner, neighbor, boss, children, friends? How about now? Are you using that anger and fear to go forward and make changes—or is it holding you back?

With either investment, what has the outcome been? Have your choices made you and those around you happier and more secure? Or have you seen a different result?

Next, look honestly at our culture at large. We need to ask the questions that beg to be answered. Is our anger working for us? Or are we suffering deeply from anger blow-back? Why are we so violent toward others—or toward ourselves? Why are there so many hotheaded, impulsive people in our culture?

Why does the slightest provocation make us blow? What devices have we rigged up in our lives that make it so easy to explode? What fuses are already lit before we go out the door each morning? Why do we light them to begin with? Where does our anger come from? How do we wrongly justify it? Is stress tipping us over the edge?

If we look closely at our heritage, we see that we've been conditioned for a long time to be combative. We've been a kick-butt, get-what's-due-me kind of culture since our nation's birth. Our severing from the British was bloody and prolonged, while

Canada somehow managed to carve out its independence peacefully.

Angry people, from George Patton to George Wallace to George W. Bush, keep cropping up in our history.

Is angry, combative, steamed-up behavior really a noble response? What about vitriolic, argumentative people, like many of our TV broadcasters? Many people think they're bold and courageous. Where do we get these ideas? Are they sound? How well do they really serve us?

What if we'd been conditioned instead by our teachers, family, clergy, and the media to believe that Jesus' fierce heart, St. Francis of Assisi's gentle strength, or Gandhi's self-mastery of his anger were really the ultimate forms of courage? Aren't they also forms of strength? Absolutely, says Berkeley peace studies professor Michael Nagler, author of *Is There No Other Way? The Search for a Nonviolent Future.*

"The capacity to stand up to a bully and the capacity not to act like one—the strength of character to rise above anger, even if that anger is perfectly justified—are closely connected," Nagler writes. "These qualities not only can coexist, they explain each other: strength is strength."

This is the kind of fierce strength of character we need to celebrate and cultivate if we're going to bring people together in our increasingly diverse world. Think Jimmy Carter. Think Mother Teresa. Think Kofi Annan.

Nelson Mandela displayed this kind of strength in negotiating with F.W. DeKlerk. At first, when DeKlerk made him angry, Mandela attacked him. But then, "I swallowed my pride" for the sake of their negotiations, he said. Maybe that's not swallowing pride but a brilliant display of pride, humility, and humanity.

Where are the Nelson Mandelas in public office, business, and other leadership positions today? Why do we insist that strength is strong-arming and dominating others? Why do we glorify the "good fight" when it has such disastrous results? Why do we still condition our boys to "fight like a man"? Why are too many children weaned on violence?

Lots of boys learn this lesson the moment they hit the sandbox. When Tajae Gaynor was growing up, he remembers, many of his classmates had parents telling them, "Somebody mess with you, you kick their ass." He remembers some parents showing up at school and slapping their children around if they weren't tough enough on the playground.

As a result, he and his friends often got into fights just because someone looked at them the wrong way. Gaynor would conclude, "I don't know what they're thinking, so I got to approach them."

Fights went down, and knives and guns came out. Gaynor lost a lot of friends because someone was "rushin' to blast somebody's new sneakers."

At times, we've become a "rushin'-to-blast" culture. Somebody messes with you—or even if you suspect they might— you mess with them first. Pre-emptive strikes are becoming our undoing.

This heritage isn't lost on our children. Congress found that more than 100,000 children bring guns to school each day— certainly a lot of "shock and awe" packed into that visual aid.

## Let Your Anger Take You to a Nobler Place

If you don't like your anger pattern, imprint a new one on your life. Start now. Use your anger as a positive surge of energy to create what you really want and need, beginning with yourself and moving out into the world. We need to channel our anger and choose a different way. We need to model that for our children, and show them how to retaliate with light, as Martin Luther King Jr. did.

During the fierce struggle for racial equality, King was routinely harassed and threatened. Then, when King and others used bus boycotts to bring Montgomery, Alabama, to a virtual standstill, the city's white founding fathers got desperate—and deadly—as they sensed their power base slipping away.

At first they tried intimidating King, questioning his integrity and leadership and telling him that the bus strike would be resolved if he was willing to step aside. They instituted a "get-tough" policy and arrested King on a trumped-up traffic violation.

Shortly after King was released from jail, someone bombed his house. He rushed home, not knowing if his wife and baby daughter were there at the time of the blast.

Can you imagine your state of mind in such a world-grinds-to-a-halt moment? Stunned disbelief? Total, paralyzing shock? Go-for-the-jugular rage? Or a combination of these?

That's why revisiting King's response is such a satisfying feast for the soul. By the time King reached his house, the mayor, police commissioner, reporters, and an angry black crowd were already swarming on his front lawn. This was one of the first open, raw displays of angry, seething African Americans ever seen in America.

King soon discovered his wife and daughter had been away during the bombing. But as the ominous crowd of black men surrounded the white reporters and town leaders, King knew that what he did at that moment could affect the arc of their anger. He knew he held the power to fan the fire or extinguish it.

King made his decision in less than a minute. He stepped out onto his front porch and asked the crowd to come to order. When there was complete silence, he spoke quietly. "We believe in law and order. Don't get panicky. Don't do anything panicky at all. Don't get your weapons. He who lives by the sword will perish by the sword.

"Remember that is what God said. We are not advocating violence. We want to love our enemies. I want you to love your enemies. Be good to them. Love them and let them know you love them."

People were stunned and relieved beyond words. Many men, their eyes shining with tears, called out, "We're with you all the way, Reverend." The entire crowd went home peacefully.

What a noble moment. That was leadership of the highest kind. Can you imagine hearing such refreshing words now? Don't retaliate; love them. Be good to your enemies. How soothing would that be to our frayed nerves? Wouldn't that uplift souls dispirited by too much trauma in the world?

King knew that he couldn't bully and crush others if the civil-rights movement was to gain momentum. A student of Gandhi, King knew retaliation always backfired, as we see everywhere, daily.

## Use Your Anger as a Guide

As King illustrated, you can use your anger as a navigating force. It can point the way to your most skillful response in any situation. Anger is often natural, even appropriate. We often get angry for a good reason. But seek to know why, when, and how you get angry. Get conscious of your hot buttons and anger triggers. Then, realize that you control your anger, not the other way around.

You can transform your anger just as you can your demonizing. You can use your anger to lead you to the heaven you seek.

We all tend to get angry and afraid when traffic is tight, work is pressured, and there never seems to be enough time to do what needs doing. Sometimes our own children can make the calmest of us go to code red. We're only human.

There's no dearth of things to be angry about in our world. Many people are angry that greed and self-interest are hurting our environment. Others are furious that they aren't getting what they see as a fair shake in life. Others are angry because their calls for calm and reason were not only ignored but often ridiculed.

We understandably get angry in life. But we can use that anger for the good of humanity, not for more madness. We can use our personal anger not to cloud our judgment and destroy our dreams but to think clearly and act constructively, as King did.

He openly wrestled with and became conscious of his own anger. He was no saint, and he didn't want to be painted as one. King admitted that controlling his anger was, at times, so hard it tormented him.

He described how he almost broke down under the "continual battering" in his community. At times, he had deep regrets when, in anger, he spoke hastily and resentfully to white leaders.

Who can't relate to that? We all say and do things in anger we later wish we could take back. "Yet I knew this was no way to solve a problem," King said. He showed that channeling his anger was a daily, hourly, second-by-second choice.

The night his home burned, his anger flared back up when it began to sink in that his wife and baby could have been killed. He became even more livid when he recalled all the hateful things that had been said about him and the black community in the previous weeks. "I was once more on the verge of corroding hatred. And once more I caught myself and said, 'You must not allow yourself to become bitter.'"

Such an enlightened concept. He could allow himself to make the choice to stay angry or bitter—or move to something greater. King showed he could allow his best self to emerge. What if we allowed ourselves to be that magnificent? What if we chose to transform our own anger into something nobler? What if we allowed ourselves to believe that we can find that kind of peace again?

King made his choice to channel his anger. What will we choose?

# Befriend Your Anger to Understand It

You can't be a peacemaker if your core is riddled with anger. Remember what Colman McCarthy said: "Peace is as much about getting the bombs out of our own hearts as out of the Pentagon budget."

The first way to defuse your anger is to understand what it's all about. We've invested a lot of shame and fear in hiding our anger. Perhaps that's one reason why fanatics, fundamentalists, and zealots can't stop fighting. Maybe they're locked into cycles of violence, shame, and the self-loathing that comes with both.

Don't run from your anger. Reflect on, befriend, and get to the root of your feeling. Don't try to suppress it. Instead, be mindful that your anger needs you to pay attention. Breathe to stay centered, and listen to what it wants to tell you. "Embrace your anger with a lot of tenderness. Your anger is not your enemy; your anger is your baby," says Thich Nhat Hanh.

Ask yourself, "What is it I need to do?" or "Why am I in so much pain?" or "Why did I get so angry to begin with?"

Think of your anger as a welcome signal from a friend. It carries a message. It's trying to get your attention. What is it trying to tell you? If you just ignore the root of your anger and act impulsively on the raw emotion of it, you can harm others. But if you pay attention to your anger and respond thoughtfully, you can transform your anger into passion and soul force and add incredible goodness to the world.

Maybe many people are quick to anger because they're nursing deep sadness over what they've had to sacrifice—pieces of their childhood. Does this strike a chord for you? How often could your anger at your boss, your spouse, children—the world—stem from the fact that you thought your world would be different?

Have you abandoned some of your ideals and dreams for a harsher reality? Is what you once held up as precious and desired now barely a memory? That would make anyone angry—and sad and scared, too. It's time to let the sadness, the despair, the shame, the anger go. Let it all go.

Now, this is key: As you release those emotions, look deeply into your heart. It holds answers for your new path. "Follow your anger; it will take you to what you love," author Matthew Fox says.

Forgive yourself for the times you used your anger inappropriately. Vow to stay more conscious next time. Look ahead to new, more positive choices that will give you more of the life for which you've longed.

What do you really desire? Ask your heart, "What do I really need in order not to feel so resentful? What do I really need in order to be filled with joy?"

## Rediscover Your Humanity

Like gardeners, says Thich Nhat Hanh, we can use our anger as compost to build a beautiful garden. "With the energy of mindfulness, you can look into the garbage and say, 'I am not afraid. I am capable of transforming the garbage back into love.'"

Try this experiment. The next time you get angry, stop before you act on that raw anger. Just stop and be with that fury. Realize how angry you are. Then close your eyes and try to direct that force toward what you really want. Use that strong energy, that heightened emotion, that intense power to visualize and ask for what you absolutely long to see in your life. With your thoughts, feed the loving wolf inside you, not the violent one.

We can use our anger to choose love, to choose a larger life. This is what turned his life around, says Roger Haeske, a successful performance coach.

For too long, he was angry with his boss. Even after he no longer had to work with that person, Haeske still felt subconscious anger lingering. Who hasn't been in a similar situation? Just when you think you've finally buried your anger, it keeps showing up.

Haeske knew his anger was impacting his work and making him unhappy. He felt he couldn't be his true self. Believing that "all consciousness is one," Haeske felt his anger hurt not only him and his former supervisor but everyone, attracting even more negativity to his life. So Haeske decided it was time to finally clear his anger. "I began to visualize my former boss and imagine him being very successful and happy. In my visualizations, I sent him a message of acceptance, divine love and well-being in every way. I simply ignored any faults and focused only on the positive."

Haeske also chose to treat his former boss as he tries to treat everyone, "as a very special person, as if I were actually speaking to God."

By watering the seeds of his love and caring, not his seeds of anger—as Thich Nhat Hanh teaches—over time, Haeske totally got rid of his anger. He now believes his anger was actually a good thing because it gave him a sense of new urgency and propelled him to move on and start his own business as a coach.

"Without this anger and discomfort, I wouldn't have made nearly as much progress toward my dreams."

## Use Your Anger for Momentum

That is the ultimate gift of your anger. Anger can lead you directly and powerfully to your dreams. If we can mindfully sit with and understand the immense force of our anger, if we can then let it lead us to what we really love, we can find deep inner peace.

Is anything you cherish calling to you? What are your ambitions? Once those answers become clear, you already have tapped into a greater power. You already are leaving your raw anger far behind; you're deep into transforming it into something higher and more supportive of you and your dreams.

Coming to peace often demands that we excavate our dormant dreams to see if our present unrest is actually smothering those unmet dreams. Think of your anger as a signal that you need to find greater balance by paying attention to your deepest needs.

Look at the underbelly of the last time you were livid. Any fear sitting there? Anger is often fear wrapped in a different box. And we were born into a society that doesn't value fear. We're told early on to stop crying, buck up, get over it, which usually means stuffing your emotions.

Could at least some of your anger really be fear? Were you road-raging yesterday because you were afraid you were going to be late for work? Were you furious when your teenager broke curfew because you were afraid she was in danger? Are you constantly angry, afraid, and ashamed because you fear you'll never be able to manage your anger and continue to hurt the people you care about?

Are you furious and scared because there are too many demands on you, and you can't begin to meet everyone's expectations? In our full-tilt society, those are common, shared emotions these days, aren't they?

Maybe your anger is so strong because you thought your life would be different, better somehow. Did you think you'd be happier, less stressed, financially stabler, and better able to live your passion? Did you assume you'd be more content than you are? Are you afraid you may never get whatever it is you want more than anything else in the world?

Usually behind any hot anger is a burning desire. What do you need? What do you desire that you fear you will never have? What's your big dream? Maybe you're afraid that what you want will never be realized. Start to separate your anger and frustration from your hopes. Focus on your dreams, on the hope, not the anger, not the fear.

It's fascinating how often in history dreams have been used to overcome anger. When the parties in negotiations or peace talks can stop focusing on their differences and turn to gaze at their common dreams, the negotiations move to the highest possible level. Jimmy Carter was a master at this.

In 1979, Carter brought Egyptian President Anwar Sadat and Israeli Prime Minister Menachem Begin to Camp David to try to resolve their differences. Begin and Sadat each came up with a list of their desires/dreams and a separate list of their outstanding differences. With negotiations and frank discussions, the second list got shorter and shorter.

But a major sticking point with Begin was Sadat's insistence that all Israeli families leave the Sinai Peninsula. Begin felt the Jews had a right to stay in the area; Sadat was angered that Begin wanted land more than peace.

Their conversations often got painfully personal and raw, Carter remembers. The men got angry, which was understandable. But they kept coming back to the table. Day after day, Carter and his advisors revised and presented new drafts of a Middle East agreement to the negotiating teams from both camps.

"On the eleventh day, however, I finally realized we faced failure because of just two issues: the dismantling of Israeli settlements in the Sinai and the status of the city of Jerusalem," Carter said. He also realized it would soon be time to return to the White House. Carter told everyone he would return to D.C. on the 13th day, basically setting a deadline for the negotiations. Not long after that, the Israelis were packing to leave Camp David.

At that point, "Something unexpected, almost miraculously helped to break the deadlock," Carter recalled. "We had made some photos of the three of us, and Begin had asked me to sign one for each of his eight grandchildren. Sadat had already signed them. My secretary suggested that I personalize them, and on each photograph I wrote in the name of one grandchild above my signature."

Carter then personally walked over to Begin's cabin to deliver the photographs. He found Begin there, sitting on the porch, "very distraught and nervous because the talks had finally broken down at the last minute."

"I handed him the photographs. He took them and thanked me. Then he happened to look down and saw that his granddaughter's name was on the top one. He spoke it aloud and then looked at each photograph individually, repeating the name of the grandchild I had written on it. His lips trembled, and tears welled up in his eyes. He told me a little about each child, and especially about the one who seemed to be his favorite. We were both emotional as we talked quietly for a few minutes about grandchildren and about war."

Carter said he sensed that Begin was thinking about his responsibility to his people and about what happens to those children in war. He was thinking of a better life for them. "Both of us had tears in our eyes. He promised to review the language of my latest revisions."

Soon after that, Begin called Carter. He would accept the compromise proposal. Focusing on the dream of a more peaceful world won out over agonizing over the bitterly divided one.

## Use Your Anger for Liftoff

Think about what your anger can do *for* you, not *to* others. Think of your anger as a tool you can use to become your best. "Anger is like rocket fuel," says counselor and author Martha Beck. "It's very potent, but it has an unfortunate tendency to explode if not handled correctly. It's also highly toxic. Swallow it, lose track of it, or store large quantities in your vicinity, and you're asking for trouble.

"Throwing it around carelessly or dumping it all over people can also have very unpleasant consequences. But once you learn how to harness it, you'll find that anger has enormous power to change your life for the better."

This allows you to be authentic with your anger and not suppress it or deny it. Now you can harness it as fuel to launch your life, your dreams, your hopes. This empowers us to use our anger not to control or destroy others, as our leaders often do, but to care for others and create change that serves our collective good.

Tajae Gaynor, who grew up on the streets of the Bronx, found he needed to feed his loving wolf. Gaynor's friends O'Neal and Ed had argued, and then O'Neal left and came back with a knife and stabbed Ed. The hospital was only two blocks away, but Ed, 17, died in the cab on the way. O'Neal, 18, got a life sentence.

To this day, Gaynor says neither he nor any of his friends who witnessed the fight can even remember what the two boys were fighting about. "Nobody. I don't remember. None of my friends there remember."

Gaynor woke up and realized his anger could either be lethal or used as a force for positive change. He took the fierce energy of street fighting and focused on what he really, really wanted. He wanted safe streets for loving children. He also wanted to stay alive. To do both, he realized he could no longer launch preemptive strikes. He had to instead channel his fury into purposeful action.

Gaynor became a conflict-resolution mediator. He got a degree in forensic psychology from John Jay College of Criminal Justice and now helps children stop fighting and get to the root of their anger. He shares a huge message that we all can use to shift-shape our anger from pain to pleasure: Learn about yourself. Get to know your own needs, Gaynor advises. Make your stake in peace personal. "Because if you understand yourself, if you understand your dreams, your aspirations, all the things that you want to do, then you'll be able to act differently when you get into conflict. I can definitely say that, because that's what saved my life—realizing what I wanted to accomplish."

Like Gaynor, we can only begin with ourselves. We can only understand ourselves, our dreams, our ideals, our passions. We can only heal our own anger before we tackle the anger of the world.

# Practice Channeling Your Anger

Practice making positive choices with your anger. Think of these choices as three steps across a bridge, says peacemaker Naomi Drew, author of *Hope and Healing*. The first step is awareness, noting our own reactions when we get angry, Drew says. Be an observer, not a reactor. "What happens in your body when your child does something that makes you mad? For many of us it starts with a quickening of the pulse and a surge of energy that makes us want to lash out."

Think about your reactions the last time you got angry. What happened inside your body? What thoughts came into your mind? Then, instead of saying, "I will never get this angry again," which many of us tell ourselves, notice your anger when it rises. Notice, and take a step back.

"The greatest tendency is to move forward into the anger, allowing it to infuse our words and actions. Inevitably, the conflict and level of anger escalate as a result," Drew says. "Our children or partner reacts to our reaction; we react back, and a small spark becomes a raging fire. It doesn't have to stay this way."

Instead of heading into the anger and fanning the fire, step back. Notice your reaction, and then breathe—not shallow breaths, but deep, abdominal breaths. Notice, breathe, and relax, even for just a few seconds. As you breathe, detach from the fire you almost stepped into.

Detach. This is the first step onto your bridge. Slow down your initial reaction to anger, "not by any means to lose the intensity of the feelings, but to convert those valuable feelings from fear, panic, or resentment into determination," says author Michael Nagler.

Then we can take the next step on the bridge, where we realize one, powerful thing: We have choices. Too often, anger fuels what we do, grips us by the throat, so we say or do things we later regret. We make over-the-top threats or say mean things or hurl insults.

When we observe ourselves instead and take a step back, "we remove the grip of anger one finger at a time," Drew says. "By detaching from our reactions, we can then choose what we are going to do next instead of being driven by that adrenaline surge."

As we detach, we can do something to cool off, because no conflict is solved in the face of hot emotions, Drew says. You can splash cool water on your face, go for a walk, eat a cold peach, look at the sky, write in a journal, or watch a funny movie. For many people, doing something physical is the best way to detach from their anger.

Being able to manage and transform our anger is empowering. Like Martin Luther King Jr., Gandhi knew the struggles—and the rewards—of directing his anger. "It is not that I am incapable of anger, for instance, but I succeed on almost all occasions to keep my feelings under control. Whatever may be the result, there is always in me conscious struggle for following the law of nonviolence deliberately and ceaselessly.

"Such a struggle leaves one stronger for it. The more I work at this law, the more I feel the delight in my life, the delight in the scheme of the universe. It gives me a peace and a meaning of the mysteries of nature that I have no power to describe."

We all can practice working with our anger so it better works for us. Even Arun Gandhi, grandson of perhaps the most famous peacemaker in the world, needed coaching and practice to channel his anger as a young man.

When Arun was 12 and Mahatma Gandhi was struggling to ease the tensions between India and Great Britain, Arun was struggling with his obsession to beat up a group of boys who regularly attacked and humiliated him.

"I was living in South Africa, and European African teenagers attacked me because I wasn't white. Native African boys targeted me because I wasn't black. I had so much anger building up inside me. I started doing all kinds of body-building and subscribed to body-building magazines. I wanted to be ready to defend myself."

His anger, Arun says, was dangerous. If he unleashed it, it would have been destructive and hard to control. Violence always careens out of control. Fortunately, Arun's parents saw how consumed with rage he was and sent him to live with his grandfather in India. The minute Arun met with his grandfather and told him about the beatings he'd endured, Mahatma Gandhi embraced him. He gave him sustenance to look at the root of his anger.

Mahatma Gandhi explained that the boys who hurt Arun had acted out of ignorance. "He told me that my 'eye-for-an-eye' revenge was not justice. He said that 'justice is when you are able to change people from their wrong ways through love and dialogue,'" Arun remembers.

## Use Your Own Humanness for Change

Gandhi also taught his grandson to tap into his anger as a positive, powerful source of energy. He spent 18 months showing Arun how to channel his emotions and energy, transform his hurt and humiliation into a healing force.

Arun learned how to rely on the force of nonviolence to transform tension in his own life as easily as drawing in the strength of each breath. The key to resolving any conflict is to know that it can be eased, shifted, and totally transformed by love and respect, Arun now teaches around the world.

"When we live with nonviolence as our foundation, we use anger positively...We begin to build good relationships with each other, with all humanity, and with nature. We learn that revenge is not justice, but reformation is."

Arun now channels his passion for peace, meeting with people all over the world who seek to lay down their anger. "Anger only succeeds in injecting fear, and when control is gained through fear rather than respect, that form of control can't last. So you have to keep escalating the level of fear to maintain control, and then we reach a stage when we cannot escalate it any further, and we create an even more dangerous conflict."

If you don't like that kind of danger, see that you can choose to start over. It's that simple. Even when you still lose it and act on your anger inappropriately—you will; it happens—just begin again, resolving to be more conscious the next time. If necessary, apologize and make amends, then start over, stay steady, and return to a more loving place.

"We are one blink of an eye away from being fully awake," says Pema Chodron. "You can feel as wretched as you like, and you're still a good candidate for enlightenment. You can feel like the world's most hopeless basket case, but that feeling is your wealth, not something to be thrown out or frowned upon. There's a richness to all of the smelly stuff that we so dislike and so little desire."

Use all your smelly things, your anger, your fear, and use them as riches to awaken compassion for yourself and others. We all get angry. We all get afraid. And now we can transform those responses we don't like. Forgive yourself, apologize and make amends as needed, and begin to make entirely new choices.

Do whatever works best to help cool your anger. Then, when you've cooled down, you can come back and talk. You can appropriately and respectfully tell the other person just how angry you are without becoming ballistic, Drew says. Or you can take another step back until you know what you want to say or do. Or even give the other person time to think about what he or she just did.

When you tell someone how angry you are, remember to use "I" messages, Drew says. Instead of saying, "You are such a jerk; you are always leaving your dirty clothes around," say, "I get frustrated because we agreed that you would be responsible for your own clothes." Or "Look, I am mad because I am tired and hot, and the last thing I looked forward to at the end of the day was seeing your dirty laundry."

View your anger as a sign that you need to make some new choices, maybe align with some new priorities and people, and take action to change a life that isn't working.

Continue to focus on your dreams and tell yourself that they can always stand up to your fears. That's what dreams are made of. The positive, higher energy of our dreams can always transcend and transform the negative, denser energy of our fears and anger.

Keep remembering that it's always possible to transform your anger into love. This is what we are hardwired to do—always to move back into our natural state of love. Instead, too often we circle around like porcupines trying to make love, trying to avoid the barbs we each can sling, says author Sam Keen.

It helps to remember that fierceness—not violence, but fierceness—is often a deep expression of what we really love. "Sometimes what looks like a fight is only the fierceness of love," Keen says. "As we move tentatively toward reconciliation, it is helpful to remember that anger is a necessary part of the dance of love."

## Channel Your Frustrations into Social Action

Many people say they're hesitant to calm their anger and give up that fire in their belly. They believe that fire gives them their edge, makes them more powerful and in control. Make no mistake. If you're a peacemaker, you don't give up your inner fire—you direct it and draw from it.

You use that fire creatively, imaginatively, powerfully as a visionary force for transformation. You use that strong passion to bring about change, sometimes sweeping changes. Many master peacemakers today are so successful because they learned how to take their angst and channel it into direct, positive, social action.

We can do the same. What issues most call to you? What injustice gets under your skin the most? Again, use those feelings as your guide.

Elissa Tivona often got angry. She got mad because people repeatedly told her that peace in the Middle East would only happen if the Palestinians just laid down their weapons. If the Jews laid down their weapons, they would always be annihilated, she was told. But if the Arabs would just lay down theirs— thankfully, at last, peace.

Tivona, a Jewish woman from Colorado, couldn't buy this argument, this same, tired, pessimistic drama. She was convinced there had to be people, Jews and Arabs, willing to come together as partners for peace in the Middle East. Where are the partners, she wondered? Where are my kindred spirits?

Her own socially conscious roots had convinced her that solidarity among people was a powerful thing. As a teenager growing up in New York, Tivona was full of idealism and hope that she could make the world a better place.

Active in a youth organization that drafted and proposed legislation for the common good, she found kinship with other students also convinced the world was theirs for the making. "This was a little capsule of time when we believed that all was possible."

Later, Tivona became involved in the civil-rights and feminist movements. She was a woman who exercised her power. She saw that she could indeed make a deep difference.

So it was especially disheartening, years later, when her own Jewish community seemed to reject her. Most people passionately, some vehemently, disagreed with her when she shared her feeling that Israeli and Palestinian partners in the Middle East could bring about peace.

Even her friends were often hostile. Finally, living in Denver and working for Middle East peace in the 1970s, Tivona and others received death threats. Her dreams were blindsided by this threat of violence. She was angry, sad, and understandably afraid to continue her work.

Painfully, Tivona withdrew from her intention of being an active peacemaker. "I decided to stay ignorant....I didn't want to look too closely. I didn't want to examine my anger."

For years, she dumbed herself down, Tivona remembers. "I went into denial. I decided that I didn't have any answers anymore. Whenever anyone asked me how I felt and what should be done in the Middle East, I just said, 'I don't know. I have no answers.'"

Nursing her anger, she became deeply estranged from her community. Actually, she wasn't even sure who her community was.

But about 10 years ago, Tivona realized it was time to end her long period of silence and reclaim her voice. She tried to look at her resentment and disappointment, to see if she could transform them. Could her emotions be used as catalyst for change? Was there still a hopeful, new way out there—beginning with her?

Tivona studied and carefully traced the threads of conflict in the Middle East. She started new conversations within the Jewish community about the idea that still called to her heart: partners for peace.

Once again, some people argued there were no such partners. "They don't exist," she was still told, and Tivona's anger flared again. But this time, she chose not to let her anger overshadow her power. She got fierce with purpose, not rage.

"I finally rebelled against the dissonance created by Israeli government policies. Fed up with mainstream propaganda claiming, 'There are no true partners for peace,' I decided to find out for myself."

Nothing would ever be the same again. "Late one night, I sat down at my computer, called up Google, typed in 'Middle East peace,' and decided that I wouldn't stop until I exhausted every entry and every single link on this topic....Now, hundreds of hours later, I have not exhausted the threads of the search yet. Not only that, but I've come across any number of partners, many of whom are Palestinian, many Muslim, many Jewish, countless Americans.

"There are hundreds of thousands of partners. These partners are worldwide, energetic, and very much present....If you go one level below Arafat and Sharon, you will find people who have been talking and reaching out to each other forever."

Setting the intention to lay down our anger and reach for peace doesn't have to be so hard. Like Susan Collin Marks, Tivona likes to use the word *spaciousness* when thinking of peace. Do what feels good, she says. Simple happiness is the most fundamental, deepest peacework.

Maybe what makes you happy is prayer. Maybe it's new friends. Maybe it's volunteering in your community, helping build a Habitat for Humanity house, or attending a peace vigil. Comedian George Carlin's proposed solution for world peace is 24-hour-a-day compulsory folk dancing!

Alan Cohen suggests sleeping for world peace. (Don't laugh. It actually seems a visionary idea in a sleep-deprived culture!) Sleeping for world peace. "Hmmm. Has sort of a nice ring to it," Cohen says. "Sometimes the most powerful action you can take toward solving a problem is to step back and allow the healing power of nature to take its course. If you try to fix something from a position of fear, anger, confusion, victimization or self-righteousness, you will not be effective."

Pray, dance, sleep, breathe, walk. From your own ingenuity, creativity, and good-heartedness, choose what form of peace expression calls to you. After "Googling" for peace totally changed her world, Tivona found herself connecting with others who shared her vision, and they organized the Perspectives on Peacemaking conference.

The event featured people working for peace from all over the world. Some of the participants were Israelis and Palestinians from the Forum for Bereaved Families, new partners for peace in the Middle East. Tivona had indeed found her community of kindred spirits.

"It was as if I had been swimming upstream for years, and suddenly I made a shift and walked over here and encountered a whole stream of people going in the same direction. People who, like me, believe in and are going toward new possibilities for conflict resolution. People who are learning and teaching and showing that it can be, and now they have the stories to tell."

Whatever works best to release your anger—peacefully and lovingly—do it. Only then can you bring your best self to the world. If we allow our anger to lead us to what we love, we can better serve others. We can light a new path.

Something absolutely unexpected, if not miraculous, happens when we get clear about who we really are and what we need and then lay those dreams on the negotiating table. It makes one wonder what could still happen in the Middle East, Africa, and all over the world if more dreams were shared.

Jimmy Carter says that historians have found there are usually only two conditions under which leaders risk going to war: Either they're highly confident they'll win, or they're concerned more about what will happen to them if they don't fight than if they do.

The latter is grounded in fear, and fear dominates too much of our daily lives. It certainly is the foundation of too much of our foreign policy. Fear is not making the world safer or more stable.

Giving into our anger and our fear is self-defeating and demoralizing. Choosing to channel those emotions into something more nourishing is critical.

You don't need to do something as sweeping as founding a new organization or marching on your government. But you may be willing to hold the peace in your grocery store, school lunchroom, office, or city streets. Whatever you find enjoyable will calm your own anger and inject much-needed love into the world.

Be patient with yourself. Practice lightly and skillfully. This isn't learned overnight. We'll continue to lash out in anger despite our best commitments to peace. We'll have setbacks; we're only human, but with mindful practice, we can master this.

Pema Chodron says, "All over the world, everybody always strikes out at the enemy, and the pain escalates forever. Every day we could reflect on this and ask ourselves, 'Am I going to add to the aggression of the world?' Every day, at the moment when things get edgy, we can just ask ourselves, 'Am I going to practice peace, or am I going to war?'"

What's your choice?

# WHAT MORE CAN YOU DO?

- **Do Personal Disarmament**

The only way to stop wars is to start with yourself. "The only way to get and stay peaceful is to concentrate on what brings you peace and resist the downward spiral of negative emotions that blames others for your lack of peace," says Dr. Christiane Northrup.

- **Stop Watching Angry, Violent Television**

Many TV broadcasts make you even more scared or livid. When you feel the surge of more adrenaline, you may be tempted to act recklessly. See how much better you feel when you tune out violent broadcasts.

- **Remember That Managing Your Anger Is Rewarding**

What a cool thing to know. We find delight by managing our anger. The joy is indescribable—so much peace and good will we can't begin to put it into words. Are we ready to know that much joy? Wouldn't it be wonderful not to be ruled by your anger but to be the conscious master of it? Recall a time you kept your anger in check or channeled it to a positive use. What happened? Did you gain a sense of mastery? How did you feel? Didn't you feel great, proud, successful—more in control?

- ## Start with an Anger Inventory

Few of us feel we can set aside 18 months, as Arun Gandhi did, to focus on our energy and how we want to express it in the world. Yet we can start to get more aware of our tendencies and patterns, moment by moment. Peace starts first with each of us.

Take just the next 15 minutes to ask yourself a few questions. Be loving, but be honest.

How many times in the past few weeks have you acted out inappropriately when you were frustrated or afraid? Did it get physical? How often did you walk around shooting angry thoughts at others, even if you didn't verbalize them? How short was your fuse? In each of these moments, do you remember your choice and what happened to you and those around you? Did you scream names at your children when they disobeyed you? Did you hurt anyone, emotionally or physically? What's behind all that anger?

How did you treat yourself in your anger? Some people have a hard time expressing their anger. Maybe they feel they don't have a right to their feelings—so they internalize them and do destructive things to themselves. They eat, drink, do drugs, or simply numb out on too much TV. Or they pretend they are "Fine, just fine" and stuff their anger so it eats away at them from the inside out forming ulcers, anxiety, even heart attacks.

What about you? What does your anger look like, and is your life better or worse for it? If you lost control and lashed out in the past two weeks, how did it make you and others feel? Are your relationships still strained?

Did you vent or dump your frustrations in someone else's lap, spamming them with your toxic emotions? Did you sulk and leave others feeling sullen? Did your anger come out sideways as you muttered an insult under your breath? Did you hurt someone?

## • Choose New Patterns of Behavior

The third step on the bridge to releasing our anger is the willingness to leave old patterns behind, says Naomi Drew. Ask yourself, "Do I really want to give up my angry reactions?" This doesn't mean you'll give up your right to be angry; it's about giving up over-reactions to anger which only makes matters worse. It's about not abusing other people, not saying or doing anything that diminishes others' dignity or hurts them emotionally or physically.

If you find you have much deep-seated, chronic anger—who, me?—discover what works best for you to purge it. Be mindful about this. Anger management is a hot area these days. Be wise about what you choose to manage yours. It is presumptuous and misleading to say that one anger-releasing technique fits all, as many Web sites claim. I suspect the process of separating the angry chaff from the loving harvest we want to cultivate in ourselves is more organic, spontaneous, and guided by more than a touch of serendipity and wonder.

Do what most calls to you. I spent some time one week researching people's stories on the Internet about how they finally released their anger. Their ways were as rich and varied as our dreams. People described throwing old, chipped pottery against their stone houses and feeling totally cleansed of their anger. One woman described digging and heaving dirt in her garden to plant new flowers, burying her anger in the soil as she did.

One man's turning point happened at a lecture when the speaker shocked him by referring to anger as a "holy emotion." The speaker told him that he could turn his anger into light and that the ultimate purpose of all anger is to create more light. The man went home, sat down, wrote down and thought about all the episodes of anger he could recall. Sure enough, he saw they were really opportunities for new growth. That was the beginning of his new, lighter life.

## • Watch Peace, Like Bread, Rise from Ordinary Moments

Master moments of anger right in the moment. When the shock-and-awe bombing first started in Iraq, emotions everywhere were heightened and raw. I overheard two customers at my favorite bread shop having a heated discussion about their opposing views of the war. I watched the clerk deftly listen to both sides with compassion, smile calmly, and say, "Well, you know, like two loaves of bread, no two people are alike, and we can all share our unique views." With only that simple but wise statement, both customers were heard, and their anger seemed to dissipate and waft out the door with the aroma of fresh-baked bread.

Peace can rise, like good bread, in ordinary moments. Celebrate those moments when you helped calm frustrations, and know you can generate more.

## • Use Humor to Defuse Tension

Some people use humor beautifully to detach from anger. Mark Gorkin, a social worker and the author of *Practice Safe Stress*, has some great ideas for using play and humor to dispel our anger.

His playful, feisty attitude once transformed a volatile courtroom situation. Gorkin was serving as a juror in a trial involving a black man accused of selling cocaine to a black undercover policeman. The jury consisted of nine blacks and three whites. Tension spiked as several of the black jurors questioned the policeman's tactics, assuming that he had mishandled a piece of the evidence. Most of the blacks appeared to be leaning toward an acquittal. After fruitless attempts to influence each other's positions, the jurors took a poll and found out that the white jurors and one black juror were swaying in the opposite direction.

"Well, it seems that the white folks and this one black guy are holding us up!" one black juror yelled. In an agitated, loud voice, the black man in question yelled back, "Just what you are trying to say?" The room crackled with tension, and the forewoman seemed paralyzed. Another black woman with long braids blurted out, "This is ridiculous. All we are doing here is pulling our hair out."

The electricity in the room jolted Gorkin to action. He shouted, "Hey, that's not fair. You have a lot more hair than I do!" The whole room burst into laughter. The forewoman said, "Guess we needed that. Now, let's get back to the facts of the case." The jurors did so, but in an easier, more respectful and tolerant manner.

## • Follow Your Anger to What You Love

As Tajae Gaynor and Elissa Tivona, Martin Luther King Jr. and Mahatma and Arun Gandhi have shown us, channeling your anger is not about suppressing, denying, or hiding it. It's about gathering and using its power to work for the common good. Instead of unconsciously scattering that energy in destructive ways, we can consciously direct it toward something more healing and powerful.

# *Five*

# GRIEVING OUR LOSSES

*I*n our perpetual feel-good culture, grief is considered an unlikely ticket to peace. Feeling sad? Isn't that the root canal of all emotions? Who wants such raw, exposed vulnerability?

We desperately try to sidestep grief as if it were a vacation stop on the road of life that we could choose not to book. But if peace is our ultimate destination, grieving our healed wounds is one of the most natural and powerful paths. If we want to activate our hearts and bring them to bear on any conflict, our hearts can't be hard and bitter with unresolved pain.

Beneath any anger is usually a story that's not been heard. Beneath any great rage is usually a loss that hasn't been fully mourned.

Mourning is a powerful salve for still-open emotional sores. It opens our hearts to listen to our own suffering and connects us to the suffering of those around us. Grieving well can connect us to our fierce inner power and make us feel strong kinship with our fellow human beings.

We will never find peace in our own beings or relationships or with other cultures and communities if our hearts are heavy with grief.

Grieving well makes us freer and lighter. It helps us find the blessings in our loss. Our sadness can transform us into someone nobler, more kindhearted and powerful.

If we embrace our sadness and pain, just as a parent embraces a child, we relieve and transform the pain, says Thich Nhat Hanh. He has seen this healing transformation work with angry Palestinians and Israelis at his Plum Village community in France. There, individuals who couldn't tolerate being in the same room together become loving with one another when allowed to finally let down their defenses and grieve their losses.

"Many from the Middle East have come to our village for more than three years. All have big pain. None have known how to breathe and embrace their despair and pain. They couldn't even look at each other because their fear and anger and pain were so huge."

Israelis and Palestinians who visit Plum Village learn how to breathe mindfully, sit, eat, and walk mindfully. They practice deep, compassionate listening and gentle, loving speech "so they can empty their heart and express everything in their heart—their fear, sadness, and suffering. They can get relief because they tell how they suffer and how their children suffer. They tell how they are victims of discrimination and fear," Nhat Hanh says.

In sharing their stories, Jews and Arabs begin to see one another as human beings. They begin to see one another as brothers and sisters and believe, often for the first time, that peace is possible in the Middle East.

"They find refuge," Nhat Hanh says. "Instead of sinking into the river of suffering, they create a boat that could float on it."

Grieving well is a potent peacemaking tool. The ancients knew this. They honored depression and grief as a gateway to unparalleled emotional, spiritual, and physical strength.

This healthy view of grief resonates with many of us who, thrown overboard into an ocean of loss, find ourselves dragged into the undertow of dark despair. When we are able to stay afloat during the grieving process, as Nhat Hanh teaches, we reach the other shore stronger, wiser, and more sensitive not only to suffering but to all that is, including great joy.

Grieving well releases hidden emotional debris. It makes us feel more fully alive. It gives us confidence that we will not only enjoy all that life has to offer but serve life, as well. Here are some ways to begin to release any grief that's keeping you from being at peace:

## Tell Your Story to Someone You Value

Swanee Hunt, former ambassador to Austria, has seen the immense healing power of storytelling and compassionate listening. While ambassador, she extended her energies to help ease the Bosnian-Serbian conflict from 1992 to 1995. After the war ended, hoping to help bring reconciliation among people in the region, Hunt created forums for Bosnian women to share the stark truth of what they experienced and, hopefully, begin to heal.

Hunt recalls one of the Bosnian women, Kada, standing before a Serbian audience to share her story. Kada lived in Srebrenica, the site of the worst civilian massacre in Europe since World War II. More than 8,000 Muslims were killed in Srebrenica when Serb forces overran what had been declared a U.N. safe zone.

With this trauma still held in her being, Kada began her story. "For three years, our town was shelled until we had no electricity. Our water supply was cut off. The international community was supposed to protect us, but they didn't. Ultimately, they separated the women and daughters from the men and boys. They told the women to get on buses with their daughters, and they said our men and boys would join us on foot. But they were all massacred. They never came back.

"I lost my husband and son and every male friend or family member. After that, I would walk all night through mine fields trying to find corn to keep from starving. The solders were choosing women to be raped. This is the loss I experienced. I'm not saying any one of you is guilty. I am not saying I want you to experience anything close to what I experienced. I just want you to know the truth."

Members of the Serbian audience responded with an overwhelming outpouring of grief and compassion, Hunt recalls. "They began crying and held their faces in their hands. They asked, 'Where were we when this was happening? We were only 200 miles away!' Their depth of emotion was enormous."

After she told her story, Kada turned to Hunt and shared how cathartic the experience had been. "I now know that I can work with these people. This connection has happened."

The connection through storytelling and compassionate listening is critical, Hunt says. "It's very hard to build bridges between people if their story is locked inside of them. I don't know if Nelson Mandela could have done what he did if we hadn't known his story."

Though most of us haven't suffered to the degree that Kada did, we still carry pain that can traumatize us and keep us from experiencing the joy and inner peace we're meant to. We, too, can find sacred release and feel more hopeful about the future by sharing our stories.

Find someone to listen to your experiences without judgment or blame. Then release them. Mourn them, if necessary; honor them. See what lessons they might have to share with you. Process your pain with a trained therapist, if necessary, until you can finally release the pain that smothers you and keeps you from breathing in life.

If you deny you're in pain or look for a less-painful shortcut to paradise or mask your pain with alcohol, drugs, excessive food or work, or other addictions, you will remain in low-energy limbo. You're also giving the pain more control and power over you.

# Allow Yourself Time and Space to Heal

Unhealed grief can run amok, fester inside, and turn into rancid bitterness, shame, and hatred. The final blow: In avoiding our pain, we also set ourselves up to be drawn constantly to situations that force us to repeat that pain. We literally, consistently attract that which gives us the same, unhealed pain. "If you don't heal the wounds of the past, you will just bleed into the future," says Oprah Winfrey.

Perhaps, says Sherri Lederman Mandell, that's why bloodshed and cruelty flow so horribly in the Middle East. Many people smother their pain, sidestep the grieving process, shut down their hearts, and become emotionally frozen by hatred, she says.

"The unexpressed grief stays in the body and gets stuck there....People can turn to stone," Mandell says. "They turn to a salt pillar—like Lot's wife, always looking back, frozen, looking at their dead children, frozen with hate for their enemies, the Israelis, frozen in the past."

Mandell was forced to become intimate with how wounds, left to fester, can hemorrhage into unspeakable violence. That kind of barbarism caused the murder of her oldest son, 12-year-old Koby. In 1996, the Mandells—Seth, a rabbi; Sherri, an author—moved with their four children from Maryland to Tekoa, Israel, on the West Bank.

After a rough adjustment, Koby finally settled into eighth grade, excelled in sports, and made new friends. One day, he and a friend decided to cut school to go hiking in the *wadi*, the dry riverbed. They wanted to know the *wadi* like the back of their hands, they said.

But instead, they got to know the cruel power of hatred. Koby and his friend were stoned to death in a cave near Koby's home. Palestinian terrorists were blamed for the attacks, although the murderers were never found.

When she heard how Koby died, just days shy of his 13th birthday, Mandell remembers herself physically sensing the horror and darkness. "Within five hours of finding out Koby was murdered, I was in my bed, and some of my co-workers, five women, came to me. I said, 'What am I going to do with this evil? It's not just that my boy was killed but that he was battered and murdered in this primitive and barbaric way.'

"Koby was only in the eighth grade and was just getting pimples. He was just on the cusp...I knew that I couldn't live with that evil. I knew that kind of evil could contaminate my kids, and I didn't want to be in it. I wasn't going to put my energy there."

We all encounter darkness, whether it's evil, meanness, violence, stupidity, or bigotry. Do you join with and feed that energy, or do you choose something that transcends that darkness? That which we put our energy into, that which we feed in our daily lives has the power to either save us or destroy us.

With her son's life extinguished by hatred, Mandell and her husband knew they had to choose something life-affirming. "My husband and I felt as one. We felt that we had to do something positive not just for ourselves but for our children."

The first important choice, Mandell realized, was that she had to honor her son and surrender to the grieving process. If she didn't, the despair was so deep it could have trapped her, she says. She chose to save herself. She sat in the wound and mourned the loss of her child.

In feeling her emotions, Mandell avoided trapping her pain and later becoming paralyzed by depression, bitterness, or the total loss of hope. She was able to walk through the gateway between her grief and her transformation into a stronger, more powerful, still-hopeful woman. "Part of you chooses this transformation, and part of it is what God and people around you give you. But you need a lot of support to manifest that kind of transformation.

"I felt I had the right people around me who I could stand on, who were there for me. From the minute Koby was killed, friends came over. They took me to my bath. They got my pajamas and helped me brush my teeth. They were there when I woke up."

One friend, Valerie, came every day for a year and made eggs in the morning, "just to be there for me."

Mandell also was blessed with another friend, Shira Chernoble, an English teacher in Israel. After Koby's murder, Mandell was surprised to learn her friend had trained as a grief counselor with Dr. Elisabeth Kubler-Ross. Shira wisely guided her through the pain, Mandell says. "She came for two hours every day and sat with me. She just listened and was there for me....If you're not alone in this process, you can survive it.

"Shira gave me hope. She would say, 'You will always have this pain, but the rest of you can grow around it.'"

## Begin to Accept What Is

Accepting what is doesn't mean we have to deny our emotions or bury our sadness when life takes a turn we hadn't wanted or expected. Accept when you are in pain. Pain is pain.

Accept that this situation is making you feel emotions you may have never felt before. Sometimes events happen that bring us to our knees. Be loving with yourself. Feel your raw emotions, and move through the experience. "You can't crush your emotions; you have to experience them, and on the other side of those emotions will lie peace," author Martha Beck says.

You need to fully feel your emotions and be with them before you can heal and move on. If you don't mourn your lost dreams, inner peace will always be hard to find. This is no easy feat, of course. It sounds great on a Hallmark card but could be our life's work to master. Beck caused herself immense pain as she learned to stop thrashing against what was. When she was pregnant with her second child, the Harvard-educated woman, who had always been under intense pressure to be brilliant, found out her child would be born with Down syndrome.

When a nurse shared the amniocentesis results over the phone, Beck was shattered. "It was as if everything I had ever strived for, every hope I'd ever hoped and dream I'd ever dreamt seemed to be poised like a delicate Fabergé egg between the tips of my fingers." As the news of her child sank in and she told the nurse she would not terminate the pregnancy, "the egg fell, smashing into a million shards on the floor."

In the coming days, she was afraid of her son and afraid for him. "The bulge of my torso now seemed freakish, monstrous, grotesque. The baby inside it was broken. He was substandard. He was not what I wanted."

Most of us can relate to her experience. How often have you recoiled in horror at some monstrous, shocking moment? Are you in the middle of one of those moments now?

If we can get some distance and look at these turning points, we start to see that the greatest pain comes from our judgment of them. The scariest of all are our own dark thoughts crashing around, leaving us with nasty head wounds.

"My mind told endless horror stories about the hideous future my child and I would endure—stories that, in retrospect, are hilarious," Beck says. "If I'd known how Adam would really change my life, I'd have been overwhelmed with gratitude, not grief. His life has brought me not only enormous love but concrete rewards: adventure, relationships, money, career success," Beck says.

"I'm not saying that having a disabled child is a guaranteed funfest but that living by heart, something Adam taught me to do, yields miraculous bounty."

When we live by heart, we accept that all is well because all is of God, of spirit, of the Creator, of one magnificent love. Anything that happens, even it is deeply painful, is an opportunity to love better. It's an opportunity to find our boundless hearts, realize our connection to one another, and care for all that is, perceived imperfections and all. It's an opportunity to become grander, larger versions of ourselves.

# Use Your Grief to Bring Healing to Others

Because she was loved and allowed to grieve—with the support and kindness of others—Sherri Mandell was able to use her pain as power for something good. She kept her heart soft and compassionate. She has written a book about her experience with grief and the blessings she has discovered since losing Koby, *The Blessing of a Broken Heart*.

She has become wise. "What do you do with tragedy and pain? You either become bitter, hardened and despondent, or you go forward and try to make beauty and joy in the world."

That beauty and joy then give life and spirit to the person you've lost, "so their spirit continues on in a different form. A part of me now sees there are blessings in everything, if you allow yourself to open to them."

Grief, as painful as it can be, is a natural opening to our true greatness, power, and the blissful peace we all crave. That is the message Mandell now offers to others in need of healing in the Middle East.

Because of her own experience there, Mandell sees that countless parents and children affected by trauma and loss are still paralyzed by unhealed grief. To promote the healing process, the Mandells created Camp Koby healing retreats.

Camp Koby provides children whose parents or siblings were killed or injured in terrorist attacks with a safe, fun, and supportive environment to express their grief and anxiety. They are loved and counseled by peers, counselors, and professional therapists, as Mandell was.

Too often after a family loses someone to terrorism, the focus is placed on the person killed and their parents or spouse. Then, after a brief mourning period, children return to school and are expected to interact with their peers and teachers as if nothing happened. "The result is that deep emotional scars are left," Mandell says.

She also creates healing retreats for mothers who have lost children or spouses to terrorism. Many gather and share their stories for the first time and finally receive empathy and support from people who've experienced similar loss. They also receive professional, compassionate support.

Mandell says her daughter, Elianna, found great healing at Camp Koby after losing her brother. Elianna met another girl whose teenage brother also was also killed by Arab terrorists. "This girl's brother was lured by an Arab girl he met on the Internet. He arranged a meeting with the girl in an Arab city, and they met, and he was shot.

"Most kids couldn't handle a story like that. But Elianna and this girl could share their stories. Both girls opened to each other."

Many people say they feel sorry for her children and others in the Middle East who have experienced great loss, Mandell says. "My hope is that they are affected but not damaged by this. I hope they become bigger, compassionate people. I hope they become leaders and healers."

Remember Colman McCarthy's saying: "Peace is as much about getting the bombs out of our hearts as it is out of the Pentagon budget." Grieving well and naturally can help us finally ease the explosives from our hearts. It can help us become free.

"I will never say that my son's death is good. I miss him and mourn him too much. But I don't want to carry death like the bird that last week caught on the hood my car, thumping up and down, in and out of my vision, a symbol of pain and captivity," Mandell recently wrote in an essay.

"I want to carry death as an awareness of a bird that is free, soaring beyond the horizon of what I can see. The only way I can do that is to believe in my capacity to know. I have to believe that God has a plan, even if this plan hurts us," Mandell says.

Effectively moved through, the grieving process can release the pain we harbor that keeps us from loving, peaceful connections with others.

We all experience loss and pain. But we aren't intended to be held hostage by them. When we suffer, we must feel it fully. Then, when we have honored our loss, we can begin to move toward acceptance that this moment, like all moments, is part of what it is to be human. Though sad, loss is a natural part of life.

From this, deep peace can start to flow. This is a peace that nourishes our compassion and love for all people. This new, boundless peace is what allows the suffering of others to pierce our hearts as much as our own suffering does. This acceptance is what primes us to be powerful peacemakers.

When the Dalai Lama accepted the Nobel Peace Prize in 1989, he lifted up the heart of the world when he shared this kind of deep, compassionate peace in describing his feelings toward the Chinese, who drove the Tibetans out of their native country. "I speak not with a feeling of anger or hatred towards those who are responsible for the immense suffering of our people and the destruction of our land, homes, and culture," he said.

"They, too, are human beings who struggle to find happiness and deserve our compassion....The realization that we are all basically the same human beings, who seek happiness and try to avoid suffering, is very helpful in developing a sense of brotherhood and sisterhood—a warm feeling of love and compassion for others. This, in turn, is essential if we are to survive in this ever-shrinking world we live in."

If you grieve naturally, you can choose to let the tears flow through and cleanse you. Then you can to choose to see the delights and blessings life holds for you. You can more readily extend an open heart to others who suffer, too.

When we can develop this sense of love for all humankind, we can settle into an unshakable peace that now eludes most of our lives. We won't keep thrashing about trying to find peace. We will be peace. Our search will be over. We will hold the peace the world is aching to have right now—a peace that allows us to more easily transcend our own suffering, become compassionate healers, and ease others' suffering. We will hold a peace that

135

allows us to forgive more easily others' transgressions and move deeply into reconciliation.

# WHAT MORE CAN YOU DO?

- **Do Some Reflection**

Is some aspect of grief still locked in your being? Do you ever feel overwhelmingly sad, yet you aren't sure why? Do you have low energy, anxiety attacks, or insomnia? Do you sometimes get red-hot with anger for no apparent reason? Or do you react to simple annoyances or slights with rage?

- **Air Your Tragedies, Pain, and Losses**

Have those wounds been allowed to breathe? Have you aired them with family, friends, therapists, ministers or other compassionate souls? Have you honored and healed your wounds or denied their existence? Keep in mind that beneath most anger is a story that's not been heard. If we keep that story trapped inside, it can blind us from seeing our blessings. If we numb our pain, we also numb the sensations of joy, ecstasy, and love. We set ourselves up for heart attacks, depression, and other illnesses, researchers now find. That kind of hell is far worse than going through grief, as painful and as terrifying as it can be.

- **Grieve, Mourn, Honor Your Losses**

What is one way to begin? As it was for the people in this chapter, telling your story to a compassionate listener is one of the best first steps. Sharing what we've experienced allows our pain to breathe. It finally releases emotions we've suppressed for too long. Dr. Christiane Northrup likens this process to the treatment of an abscess. She calls it emotional incision and drainage.

"Any surgeon knows that the treatment for an abscess is to cut it open, allowing the pus to drain. When this is done, the pain goes away almost immediately, and new, healthy tissue can re-form where the abscess once was. It is the same with emotions. They, too, become walled off, causing pain and absorbing energy, if we don't experience and release them."

- **Express Your Emotions**

The opposite of depression is expression. Express your feelings through whatever method works best for you, whether it's therapy, journaling, chanting, talking to the earth in nature—whatever works best for you to most release your pain. Many people find body work and energy healing such as massage, reiki, therapeutic touch, or acupuncture extremely helpful in releasing stored pain.

- **Observe Your Pain with a Compassionate Heart**

Even if only a little, try to begin to accept what you see, just as it is. Look again at what you think blocks you from your peace. If spirit is in everything, in all the details of our world, even the ones you judge as horrible, could this, too, have a spiritual aspect to it? Is there some meaning to be found in this loss and pain?

Many people now are grieving and anxious about what appears to be madness and turbulence in the world. What if all the apparent chaos is actually evolution in the making? asks Lynn Kendall, spiritual leader at Unity Church of Fort Collins in Fort Collins, Colorado. What if the unrest is actually a call to take the world to a higher level?

"We are all spiritual leaders. I really believe that. Whatever it is that we take with us in the world—our spiritual essence, our spiritual nature—we offer up as leadership. Leadership is learning to accept chaos as necessary to spiritual creation. What if the apparent madness and everything that looks like something other than love is just an indication of our evolution?"

What if we are breaking free from old systems and values that hold us apart from God, spirit, the divine, whatever you wish to call the sacred in life? Breaking apart and letting go of old ideas and choices that no longer serve us can be messy and painful, says Kendall.

"Life is messy at times. But soon you begin to see an order that is better than before. It's about embracing chaos and walking through fear, knowing that on the other side is my highest and best.

"I want to embrace all the chaos, turbulence, and difficulties and say, 'Come on. We can do this. We can move to a higher level and become finer and better men, women and children. We can lift our consciousness and raise ourselves up.'"

*Six*

# LISTENING FOR PEACE

*L* eymah Gbowee, who helps Liberian women find some measure of peace in the middle of war, has found one powerful peace tool. "The women I work with say, 'People come with food. Others come with clothes. Some come with slippers, but you've come with the best thing for us today. You've come to listen to us from our stomach!'

"Traditionally, if a woman tells you in Liberia that you've come to listen to me from my stomach, it means that this is my innermost secret that I'm telling you, and there is no way in this world that I can tell it to anyone. And because you've come to listen to what is in our stomach, you've done the best thing that anyone else could do."

Simple, deep listening—the laying on of ears—works miracles. "Violence is the language of the unheard," Martin Luther King Jr. said.

Think of a time when you had something important to say, and no one listened to you. No one seemed to care in the least. Or maybe they cut you off, even ridiculed you. Can you remember how you felt? Frustrated, maybe? Invisible? Scared? Hopeless?

Maybe all you felt was angry, so angry you felt you could scream at or hurt someone.

Our search for peace must lead us to become better listeners. We have, consciously or unconsciously, hurt others because we haven't listened to them as deeply as they needed us to.

It's all too easy to overlook or try to hurry and "fix" others without fully honoring their stories. As Americans, we've often turned a deaf ear to people we haven't understood or agreed with, inciting even more tensions and misunderstandings. In a world full of people aching for more acceptance, how has our unskilled listening caused greater conflict?

Listening can ease much of this pain. When we listen so deeply to others that we see ourselves in them, our hearts fall open to those we judged as "other." We can see, often to our great surprise, that they are much more like us than we ever imagined.

That's why many peacemakers are now turning to a powerful practice known as compassionate listening. It's hard to stay arrogant and rigid and separate when you see a mirror held up in front of you through this kind of deep listening.

In a blinding moment of insight, once-fierce adversaries suddenly see that everyone has a story, everyone has pain and suffering, and everyone has a version of the truth. "Out beyond ideas of wrongdoing and right doing, there is a field. I'll meet you there," said the mystic Rumi. Finding that someone else's story is similar to your own helps you meet on that field.

When we see the unrest in the world today, we recognize that many souls are not resting well at all. How much of that unrest comes from not being heard? We've never fought a war and listened to both sides, says Gene Knudsen Hoffman, a pioneer in compassionate listening. We've never done it. We've always chosen what we thought was the best side that favors our viewpoint. Then we made the other into the enemy.

What a startling observation. Could we have averted any of the wars we've been in if we had listened to our so-called enemies more deeply—or at all? If we'd deployed our ears as much as our soldiers, how different might our reality be? "If we could read the secret history of our enemies, we should find in each person's life sorrow and suffering enough to disarm all hostility," Thich Nhat Hanh says.

Compassionate listening is nothing short of humanitarian aid. It heals individual relationships as well as our relationships with other nations. It offers much-needed hope when hope seems long gone. "When someone listens to you in a compassionate way that allows you to fully embrace your experience, you can survive anything. You can reconcile with any aspect of your life and let it go, when your story can be truly and deeply told," says Shawnee Undell.

The true measure of our greatness is whether we can listen to the stories of those we loathe, to whom we have surrendered our inner peace. "Listen to their stories about their childhoods and what they went through. Allow yourself to imagine yourself in their shoes....the more we hear the stories, the more we see that those who are our enemies are themselves fully human and fully deserving of respect," says Michael Lerner.

How do we begin to weave compassionate listening into our lives to ease our own tensions and disagreements? Again, it helps to see how it's already being applied in the Middle East, Africa, Bosnia, and in our ordinary conflicts here. Here are some ideas you can consider:

## Use Compassionate Listening to Honor Others

"How are we going to make it as a global family? I don't think it's possible without making this evolutionary leap into learning the skills of compassionate listening," says Leah Green, the founder of Compassionate Listening, a groundbreaking organization working in the Middle East and all over the world. Green believes that compassionate listening is "one of those bedrock skills we now absolutely need to make it into the next 'Great Turning,' as Joanna Macy calls it, or the next true era of peace."

With compassionate listening, you don't judge, correct, or try to fix anything. You don't debate, defend, or take sides. You listen to someone's story with an open heart, "creating a loving space, whether you like what they're saying or not," Green says.

We can try to resolve our differences with our brilliant minds, but unless we also engage our brilliant heart wisdom, we can go only so far in bridging our differences. Compassionate listening softens and engages our hearts, making us more willing to stretch for peace.

Green sees this happening with the hundreds of people touched by compassionate listening in the Middle East. "During one delegation, we met with and listened to the governor of Gaza. He was very official and diplomatic and gave us lots of information. He also described daily humiliations, like having to cross the checkpoints in front of the Israeli soldiers."

But as the man shared his story, he kept it on the "head level," Green remembers. Then one of the compassionate listeners reflected back to him the humiliation she heard in his story, and suddenly he shifted to his heart, his emotions. "His eyes teared up, and he became a different human being right in front of us. His face opened up. He got very soft. He started talking very much on the personal level about his own story. Listening from the heart, hearing someone so deeply you get to their core essence, who they really are, is a very honoring experience."

Being listened to well helps us make peace. It is an honorable gift that frees us all. It expands and lifts us up. It offers us the respect and love we all crave. Who among us doesn't wish to be honored by such deep listening? Who doesn't need this loving, accepting space? Can you begin to listen to others this deeply?

How well do you feel you're listened to now? How deeply do you tune into yourself? As a child, how well were you honored and acknowledged? "When I speak to a group I ask, 'How many of you felt really seen and heard as a child in your family?'" Green says. "Maybe one or two lucky people, at the most, will raise their hands. To not be seen by the people who claim to love you the most is a really painful thing. These are core wounds.

"So when someone really sees you and acknowledges your suffering, something in your soul can rest. It creates true peace inside."

Compassionate listening has to begin where we live and work. Through training from Leah Green's Compassionate Listening, Thich Nhat Hanh's community in Plum Village, France, and other organizations, rising numbers of people are weaving the practice into their daily lives.

## Listen to Reach the Root of Conflict

Viviane Ephraimson-Abt has helped students of all ages, experiences, faiths, and cultures reach greater understanding through compassionate listening at Colorado State University in Fort Collins.

The assistant director of resident and apartment life for multicultural education, Ephraimson-Abt was trained in compassionate listening by John McCluskey, a trainer for the Ojai Foundation's Center for Council Training in Ojai, California.

This huge-hearted form of listening has resolved long-standing conflicts that festered in her staff. Ephraimson-Abt manages university staff who, in turn, supervise the residential student-housing staff.

Like a mirror of our own workplaces—and a microcosm of our culture—her staff often experience a clash of cultures. By its very nature, her department is ripe for all sorts of misunderstandings among people from different national, ethnic, socio-economic, and religious backgrounds.

"In a cross-cultural community like ours, conflicts can happen because people have deeply held values, even fossilized opinions. Age is a factor because our staff is made up of graduate students. So we might have a 20-year-old with no management experience managing a 40-year-old who has worked in his or her field awhile."

With all these issues at work, compassionate listening becomes an opening to soothe hostilities, ease misunderstandings, and bring people together. "When people are able to speak their truth, without any cross talk, they are finally able to really hear each other," Ephraimson-Abt says.

Once she organized a council for compassionate listening among her staff at the middle of a school year. As they sat around in a circle, they were asked to respond to the question, "What has worked well for you this year?"

One female manager had had many conflicts that year, especially with some staff members she supervised. She felt so overwhelmed by the challenges she faced that, when it came her turn to speak, she just sat silently. But that silence sent an overwhelming, unmistakable message to the group. Many of the staff, especially those who had defied or fought her management, understood what she was saying.

"Some of her staff apologized to her because they heard in her silence how hard the year had been for her. Some of them had intentionally worked against her," Ephraimson-Abt says.

Through the practice of compassionate listening, it was easier to see with greater clarity and tolerance the root of some of the tensions. For instance, the manager was supervising people who were frustrated with their own lives, and some of them were less respectful of leadership from a woman. There, sitting in the circle, was an opportunity for them to hear her truth and do some reflection.

"Many of her staff began to apologize for their actions. They also started to forgive themselves for putting themselves in situations that didn't work for them. Some of the staff realized that they needed to make some changes. Some knew they needed a new job.

"One man, who for years had expressed his anger inappropriately and tried to gain more power, realized he was best served by leaving the university. He now has a position more suited to his abilities. It was a powerful experience to see this kind of understanding coming from the council practice."

As people struggle with their differences, compassionate listening offers an open, accepting place where "people get heard for who they are without anyone saying, 'Let's problem-solve this,'" Ephraimson-Abt says. "When you are heard on a deep level, you're offered a mirror that allows you to see yourself in a different way. When you are heard, you can hear yourself and have the possibility of asking, 'What do I think? What do I feel?'"

Ephraimson-Abt and some of her colleagues have now offered compassionate-listening and intentional-dialogue training in their community to other university staff, healthcare workers, peacemakers, government employees, and many others.

As Ephraimson-Abt has found, compassionate listening can bring deep healing to wounds that otherwise might fester for months or years. "Council and other forms of compassionate listening and intentional dialogue are instrumental in the development of authentic and healthy connections. This type of deeper communication makes it possible for each of us to bring more of ourselves fully into our family, community, and work settings," Ephraimson-Abt says.

"All of us benefit from each of us being more wholly present. As a result, our understanding of each other deepens, conflicts are resolved, and our relationships with one another become richer and more satisfying."

## It's Not about Who's Right or Wrong

Esther Sadeh has seen how listening from the heart, not the head, can help dissolve tension in the Middle East. A native of Israel, Sadeh has practiced compassionate listening in both Israeli and Palestinian-occupied territories through Leah Green's organization.

After listening to the stories of both Palestinians and Israelis, Sadeh saw that the conflict in the Middle East is not about who owns territories, buildings, and boulders. It's not about who's right or who's wrong. "It's about hatred and fear," she says.

Israelis are still haunted by fear and loss, says Sadeh, whose father immigrated to Israel from Poland before World War II. Most of his family members remained in Poland and died in concentration camps.

Many Palestinians are afraid, as well, that no one cares for or respects them. Many live in poverty and refugee camps and fear they will never have their own homes or employment again, Sadeh says. She felt the fear of her own extended family in Israel. They were stunned when she announced that she intended to enter Palestinian territories to listen compassionately to families there. "They thought I was crazy. They warned me not to open my mouth because they would know I was Israeli."

But Sadeh and her friend Barbara Lehner went anyway with their Compassionate Listening delegation to stay at the home of a Palestinian family near Hebron. Not long into the meeting, Sadeh was asked if she spoke Hebrew. She admitted she did, and the Palestinian mother grimaced at realizing Sadeh was Jewish. "They knew I was a Jewish American who knows Hebrew. They couldn't imagine that I was born in Israel because no Israeli can visit certain areas in the West Bank."

But when Sadeh and the group listened to the family's experiences and suffering, the climate shifted. The father shared his sadness that his family lived in poverty. The conflicts prevented him from going out each day to tend his olive groves, he said. By listening from the heart to the family's experiences, Sadeh felt the suspicion ease. "The tensions melted so fast. We later dined, drank, and left one another with kisses and hugs."

Even one person holding the heart space for peace can have immeasurable impacts, Leah Green says. "People are researching what happens when even one person anchors their intention through the heart. That person emanates a very strong electromagnetic field that changes the electromagnetic field of everyone in the vicinity.

"This is huge. That says that even one person can make a difference. There is some kind of magic that people feel and can't necessarily explain. But it has to do with the field we create through focusing our heart."

## Listening Eases Tensions that Could Turn Violent

Countless stories surfacing from war zones show how anchoring our intention through the heart eases tensions, often stopping violence before it breaks out. The following story came from Marion Pargaman, an Israeli social worker and group facilitator who lives in Jerusalem. Trained in the mindfulness and deep-listening work of Thich Nhat Hanh, Pargaman used the power of compassionate listening to bring peace.

Pargaman was part of an extraordinary eight-day walk that allowed Palestinians and Israelis to come together, talk, and reflect. Participants walked together from Tel Aviv-Yaffo to Jerusalem, passing Jewish and Arab towns and settlements in silence, holding a commitment to deep listening and nonviolence.

The last day of the walk was April 8, the eve of the Holocaust day, a day of deep emotion for the Jewish community. When Pargaman came to join the walk that day near the walls of the old city in Jerusalem, she saw an Arab and a Jew arguing in the crowd. The police were watching, wondering if they should intervene. Pargaman helped calm the situation. The Jewish man boarded a bus, but then a Jewish woman started to provoke the Arab man.

A Palestinian woman rushed in, assuming the Arab man was being attacked. Marion watched the woman and saw that she was "like a bomb ready to explode. I try to explain to her what is going on, but she is furious with me, screaming out her hatred, her despair and her pain.

"This is Palestine accusing Israel. At this moment, I represent Israel for her. This whole situation is greater than the two of us and takes on proportions beyond our present meeting.

"She shouts out her sorrow about what is going on now in the territories, the military incursions into Palestinian towns...She is convinced we want to kill them all. Why do we hate them so?...

"I don't try to argue with her at all. I don't show any reaction to all these accusations. I feel a huge compassion and an intense need to listen to her, only listen to her. My patience is nourished by understanding that behind this overwhelming hatred is a deep suffering and pain aggravated by the present situation of war."

As she listened, Pargaman realized that she felt calm and peaceful inside. "I know that it is the only way to calm her fury. I let her express herself for a long time without interrupting her. As she continues to shout at me, I tell her that she has no need to speak so loudly because I am listening to her with all my attention. At the same time, I find myself caressing her arm. She lets me do it and progressively lowers her voice, while continuing to let her despair overflow.

"She says to me, 'Do you understand why some of us come and commit suicide among you? You kill us anyway, so why not kill you at the same time?' She even mentions the possibility of coming and blowing herself up out of despair.

"I tell her softly that I don't want her to die. Nobody should come to this decision. We all suffer on both sides. She goes on claiming that the Zionists only want to get rid of the Palestinians. I tell her, 'You see I am a Zionist, and I don't want to get rid of you. I wish we could live together as neighbors.' She listens to me!"

Pargaman and the woman talked a bit longer, their voices calm, each of them listening easily to the other. The Arab woman was almost totally calm when Pargaman noticed the people from the mindfulness walk approaching, a hundred peaceful people walking slowly, quietly, totally in silence.

Pargaman suggested that the woman join her in the walk. As the walkers came close, one woman reached out and kissed the

Arab woman on the cheek. It appeared they knew each other, Pargaman said. "I notice that she is very moved by the walk and the atmosphere it radiates. She seems to me calmer and calmer. Nothing like the furious woman I met only minutes earlier."

The end of the line of people passed by the two women, and Pargaman prepared to join her friends. She said to the Arab woman, "I am sure that some day we will succeed in building peace between us." The woman replied, "Me, too."

Then, to Pargaman's total surprise, "She comes close to me and kisses me on my cheeks! She walks alongside the line for a while. She tells me that she likes this walk, that it makes her feel good, gives her relief, and that her mood is much better now. I am very, very moved. I feel overwhelmed by this encounter, especially by its unexpected ending. Peace was there around the corner. I did not miss it!"

Let's not miss any opportunities for peace. Peace is always possible if we just reach for it. Reaching instead for war, for bombs, for fighting displays a gross lack of imagination for anything greater. It's a horrible misuse of power.

These times call for all of us to use our power more wisely, so we, too, can seed peace wherever we are.

Our ears are mightier than we give them credit for. And by listening—listening to one another's songs of hope and suffering, joy and despair—we can appreciate that, as different as those songs may seem, we're still one, at heart. And when all our songs blend together, they create one, pure note of peace.

# WHAT MORE CAN YOU DO?

- **Ask Yourself How Well You Listen to Others**

Being listened to helps us release anger, grief, and sadness that we may have buried inside for far too long and that make us more prone to violence. When we are listened to, we feel whole and strong, and we, in turn, can offer a compassionate ear to others.

It begins with each one of us. How well do you listen to others? How comfortable are you with slowing down, sitting quietly, and breathing in another's story?

## • Listen to the Story of Someone Close to You

Practice deep listening with someone in your own home or workplace. It's great practice. Let them speak their truth peacefully and directly. Let them say what needs to be said. Stay even and calm and meet the other person's gaze. Keep your arms unfolded, away from your heart. Keep breathing, to keep your heart soft and nonjudgmental. Consciously surrender to the belief that just by listening to others, you can help and support them. Maybe you're allowing them to let go of a conflict. Maybe their inner tension can now fall away. Perhaps they will feel more energized, hopeful, and alive. Our daily path can "lead us to learn to use our gifts to heal and serve, to create peace around us, to honor the sacred in life, to bless whatever we encounter, and to wish all beings well," says author Jack Kornfield. Your listening offers all of that and more.

## • Get Trained in Compassionate Listening

Individuals, organizations, and communities everywhere are reaping amazing benefits, both personal and professional, from compassionate-listening training. So convinced of the power of this form of deep listening to resolve conflicts and bring people together, a school in Louisville, Kentucky implemented a schoolwide compassionate-listening program. The city of Fond du Lac, Wisconsin, offered compassionate-listening training to all its employees. These are just a few examples. You can create more.

# *Seven*

# DEPLOYING OUR HEARTS

W e can talk peace, march for peace, negotiate peace, and even legislate peace, but unless we hold it within our own hearts, we will never really enjoy peace. "True peace belongs to the heart," said author and philosopher Henri Nouwen.

To transform the violence in our lives, one of the most powerful but often overlooked solutions is the sheer power of love. Just as the force of hatred has kept us separate, the force of love can melt our anger and heal us. Anything is possible if we are willing to bring an open, graceful heart to our conflicts.

Martin Luther King Jr. relied on this type of humanity in healing racial tensions in the 1960s. He told his followers, "We have before us the glorious opportunity to inject a new dimension of love into the veins of our civilization." That love may be our salvation, he added. It will bring about "miracles in the hearts of men."

All of that is still true today. Who isn't ready for such a miracle? Fighting has not gotten any of us what we really want. Fighting hasn't made us free. It's imprisoned us.

We long to love better and see more tenderness in the world. We long to care for one another and be cared for in return.

Many, of course, would still argue that the instinct to be violent when we're wronged is far greater than our instinct to protect and be humane. But mounting evidence shows just the opposite. Countless research studies show that our most powerful instinct is to keep life sacred.

"We tend to think human beings have this natural tendency to kill, and yet in the middle of a hot war, WWII—a 'good war'– the U.S. army was astonished to learn that at least three out of every four riflemen who were trained to kill and commanded to kill could not bring themselves to pull the trigger when they could see the person they were ordered to kill," says negotiator and anthropologist William Ury. "And that inner resistance to violence is a well-kept secret."

Sam Gbaydee Doe, who works with child and rebel soldiers and people who have committed horrific acts, says, "I am of the strong opinion that violence is not a part of the human nature. It is a social conditioning. A lot of the people who find themselves part of the violence have fragmented lives. They haven't experienced the wholeness of themselves, their spirit, their consciousness, and their physical being. That disintegration creates the chaos that happens within them and drives them to all kinds of behaviors and attitudes that manifest themselves in violence.

"Those who perfected violence, I strongly believe they do not intend to hurt the ones who are the victims of violence. What, in my mind, they are trying to do is communicate what is happening inside themselves. They're saying, 'I'm hurt.' In their society, they haven't found a way of articulating that hurt, of expressing it."

We resist violence because we know that it is not our true nature. Being loving is our true nature. We suffer when we violate our instincts to care for others. In his achingly haunting book, *War Is a Force That Gives Us Meaning*, *New York Times* war correspondent Chris Hedges says soldiers at the moment of real battle "weep, vomit, write last letters home….all are nearly paralyzed with fright."

Hedges, who was imprisoned in Sudan, expelled from Libya, ambushed in Central America, and shot at in Kosovo, has seen how dehumanizing war can be. He has uncovered mass graves and witnessed atrocities that haunt him still. Some of his colleagues lost their lives covering wars.

War, Hedges says, is like a narcotic. And we have chosen war because it satisfies our desire for a shared sense of meaning and purpose, a cause. We discover in the communal struggle that war "fills our spiritual void," he says.

But love can also fill this spiritual void, Hedges writes. If we allow it to, love can give us the sense of shared purpose for which we long. "Love alone fuses happiness and meaning....The covenant of love is such that it recognizes both the fragility and sanctity of the individual. It recognizes itself in the other. It alone can save us," Hedges says.

The force of love so desperately needed now is not tawdry or sentimental. It is not something cheap, like reality-show couplings. It's a powerful, practical, highly effective conviction that is healing conflicts all over the world. The most experienced, trained peacemakers working in war zones are sharing that, after exhausting all their best peace tools, often it's simple compassion that finally brings heaven to the most horrific hells on earth.

Such humane approaches to conflict are the most exciting developments of our time. They reflect a form of love known as agape—a love that fully recognizes our connection to one another. When even one of us suffers from war and fighting, we all suffer. When one of us thrives, we all thrive a bit more.

Agape sees that "We were made for each other. We were made for love," as Archbishop Tutu says.

Martin Luther King Jr. used agape to heal hatred and racial tensions. "Agape means nothing sentimental or basically affectionate," King said. "It means understanding, redeeming good will for all. It is an overflowing love, which seeks nothing in return. It is the love of God working in human lives."

King knew that true compassion called forth the ultimate strength and courage. In fact, in French, the word *courage* means "to be of heart." Susan Collins Marks says, "Courage is about having a big heart, and it is at the core of peace work....It requires a big heart because it's through the heart that we communicate and connect with others. When we stand up for what we need to say, it has to be at a heart level as well as a head level."

With such courage at work in our lives, we find it easy to fully recognize the essence, the goodness, the humanity in others, even if we don't support their actions. With agape in our hearts, we may not be able to change a person's behavior, but we can change how we feel about that individual. We can trust and have faith that the love within us can lead us to greater forgiveness, understanding, and possibly a future with the people we resent, even hate.

Here is a host of ways love can bring us deeper peace:

## During Conflict, Share What Lies in Your Heart

From Ireland to Africa, we can easily find many examples of the heart overcoming hate. When even one person stands in love and expresses from the heart, that grounding in something greater allows the most unlikely reconciliations to unfold. That kind of love yields miracles when nothing else works.

William Ury has seen this in action in war zones all over the world. He was once leading a discussion between a group of Turkish and Kurdish leaders who had deep hatred for one another after fighting in a civil war for 25 years. They'd destroyed thousands of one another's villages and killed thousands of one another's families and friends. And now many of those warriors were courageously sitting down, face to face, to try to find some semblance of healing with the people they'd harmed.

Ury remembers that, at one point in the meeting, like a match exploding in the darkness, a retired Turkish admiral spoke up. "I just want to say one thing," he said. "As a member of the Turkish Armed Forces, I want to apologize to all the innocent Kurdish villagers who suffered at the hands of our armed forces during this terrible war."

All of a sudden, the room went still. "You could have heard a pin drop," Ury said. "And then the Turkish people started clapping. It was a turning point in the meeting, because his words were from the heart. There is only so much you can do from the head. Once the heart gets engaged, it makes the breakthroughs."

Love causes a "hundred veils to fall each moment," said the 13th-century poet Jelaluddin Rumi. Love removes all our veils of denial, ego, fear, and judgment, which keep us separate and unable to fall in love with the preciousness of one another. As Ury says, love makes breakthroughs.

## Embrace a Change of Heart

Just as global fighting has snapped many awake to the need for much more understanding among the world's peoples, each new conflict in your life can awaken you to the need for compassion.

Use your feelings as your touchstone, your heart's guidance. If you don't like what you're feeling, maybe it's time for a change of heart. Perhaps it's time to open your mind about this person and situation, shifting your heart in the process. Nothing you want to change in your life can change to the degree you desire unless you first change your heart about it.

You may be angry at your husband or mistrust your co-worker or hate your political leaders, business competitors, even family members. But staying with those emotions keeps you immobilized. They strip you of your true power and worth. They make you a lesser person. Be open to your feelings about your conflicts, and be open to your heart's showing you a better way.

Many people find that their religious and spiritual beliefs help reveal that better way. Rick Lunnon, a prominent Denver real estate broker and developer, was involved in a contentious lawsuit with a building and development firm, Johnson Brothers. At the time of the litigation, which dragged on for two years, Lunnon was at the midpoint of his life, approaching 50. "I was anticipating a time of semi-retirement enjoyed after a successful career, like many of us Baby Boomers born into post-war affluence. Through scholarship programs earlier in my life, I'd been granted an Ivy League education, and this blue-collar kid had a taste of blue-blood society and had enjoyed social and financial mobility.

"Business opportunity, coupled with a strong work ethic, had created affluence, and yet I was struggling with not feeling very significant, in spite of my success. I had every necessity and enjoyed most luxuries, but I was beginning to feel emptied by the vanity and senselessness of life."

At the "halftime" of God's plan for his life, Lunnon said he didn't feel anger toward the Johnson Brothers about the litigation as much as he felt haunted by a larger question, one that calls to many of us at midlife: What if I don't make my life count? What if the litigation—and all the financial resources it demanded—didn't fit with his commitment 15 years earlier to use all the resources of his life to serve the Lord?

Suddenly one day during exhaustive depositions, Lunnon asked one of the Johnson brothers about his faith. "I shared what God had placed in my heart, that the income from the litigation would be going into God's work, and that continuing litigation would only be eroding the net proceeds available for God's work.

"I challenged them to consider that continuing litigation would be wasting God's resources, including our collective time, and that there might be higher ground on which God intended for us to interact. Within hours, we came to an agreement that the settlement money would be set aside for Christian purposes."

Within weeks, Lunnon and the Johnsons found an opportunity and a region that called to their hearts: Thailand. In the three years since they settled their lawsuit peacefully, they have used their collective knowledge to help build and expand schools and orphanages for homeless and abandoned children. This humanitarian work has totally transformed their lives and those of countless others.

# Practice Thinking Loving Thoughts

Just as you practice other skills, practice using your loving thoughts, as you do your peaceful intentions, to shift the energy, climate, emotions, and actions in any given situation, no matter how volatile. That is when you realize your true ability to be a peacemaker. This is not a pipe dream. This is concerted, concentrated, disciplined work.

It will not always be easy. But, just as it's impossible for your home to feel safe if it's polluted with angry thoughts, it's impossible to create a more peaceful world if you hate political leaders, terrorists, or people you just don't know. Try seeing the essence of them. Try seeing their true natures.

What we feed with our emotions and thoughts magnifies. Use the power of your thoughts wisely. An avalanche of research shows we can't have one thought—not one, single thought—without it's somehow triggering a chemical reaction in our bodies. Chronically angry and sad people are much more likely to develop diseases.

From our heartbeats to our mood chemicals, our bodies' health and well-being are affected by our thoughts. It's only logical, then, that our thoughts and actions affect the body of the earth.

When we focus our minds and will on our love for humanity, that collective energy impacts the heartbeat of the entire earth. Give no power to violence. Don't focus on it in any way. Focus instead on what you want to grow across the earth. Look for and expect it. Seed hope.

Look for the light. We are the loving peace. We can use our power, a power obtained by acts of love, "a thousand times more effective and permanent than the power based on punishment," Gandhi said.

# Believe That Love Really Works

When we get to the real heart of any conflict, our hearts can often be softened by understanding. We usually don't want to remain angry or mean-spirited, at least on some level. We long to let our hearts soften and move more deeply into compassion.

Believe in the power of love. Be mindful of what you believe, ask for, and draw to you. Believe in the absolute best so the highest good unfolds in your life.

Loving thoughts can help transform any situation, as Louise Diamond has found. Diamond was once filming interviews in a region wracked by years of violence. After a tough day of successfully gathering footage from intellectuals viewed by the government as rebels and enemies, Diamond was euphoric. Though her piece featured interviews from both sides for balance, on this particular night, she was returning from "enemy" territory.

Diamond was just about to cross through the military checkpoint when she realized that, in her relief at having accomplished a scary and daring project, she had forgotten to cover up her video camera on the back seat. She knew that this oversight placed her and her hosts, who had driven her to the rebels, in danger.

So she activated the force of love. Holding in her mind the dignity of the soldiers on both sides, she "slipped into a place I have learned to go when things get difficult. I opened my heart to the flow of love and appreciation for all in this conflict who were struggling to find a better way.

"I saw the soldiers as whole and holy beings doing the best they could to care for their people. I saw my hosts as whole and holy beings doing the best they could to care for their people. I called on the Spirit of Peace and filled the car with her light."

As they drove up to the soldier at the gate, Diamond simply sat and radiated that light. The soldier began to question the driver sternly, looking inside the car, sweeping it with his eyes.

"When he saw me, something softened. He straightened, smiled, and waved us through."

Love is that powerful. Believe it; call on it. Mahatma Gandhi once said that love is "the only force capable of transforming an enemy into a friend." The way our nation has been alienating people of late, we dearly need more precious friends in the world.

## Commit Acts of Love

I called the acting from our hearts "radical acts of love" in my last book, *Radical Acts of Love: How Compassion Is Transforming Our World*. After you take good care of yourself, move your tenderness outward. Extend compassion to your neighbors, their children, your children's teachers, your co-workers, grocery-store clerks, doctors, and staff. Serve others from a peaceful heart. Ask to be used for a loving purpose. Thank others. Let them know you see them and their gifts.

Love wholeheartedly. It may feel awkward, even alien. You might feel exposed and raw. Be kind anyway. Say the tender words. Make the loving gesture. The peace you will impart to your workplace, organization, school, or neighborhood will be unimaginable. If you doubt that one person can make such a difference, know that, to others, your acts of compassion may make all the difference.

At 38, Kenneth Schwartz was a successful healthcare attorney in Boston at the peak of his career. But he was worried about some troubling symptoms. He not only was having difficulty breathing but also was bone-tired all the time. And what was he to make of the chronic cough and low-grade fever?

Schwartz eventually went to Massachusetts General. He was stunned when a chest x-ray revealed possible lung cancer. He was told to prepare for exploratory surgery the next morning. His blood pressure rose; his heart rate became dangerously high.

Reeling, he sat down with the surgery nurse. But he felt even worse when she was cold and brusque. The hospital felt foreign,

159

unwelcoming. It was mobbed, the nurses harried. Schwartz was terrified and breathing hard.

And then the nurse suddenly did a very small thing. She looked at him, really looked at him. And when she found out he was only 38 and had a two-year-old son, Ben, she stopped what she was doing—the briefest of pauses in the busiest of days. She reached out and held Schwartz's hand and, with tears in her eyes, asked, "How are you doing? I have a nephew named Ben." By the time she was finished with the paperwork for Schwartz's surgery, she was wiping her eyes.

Though she normally wouldn't have done so, she promised Schwartz she would see him before his operation the next morning. She kept her promise. As he lay on the bed, waiting to be wheeled into surgery, she stood with him, holding his hand, tears in her eyes. "Good luck," she said.

Schwartz's surgery revealed he had advanced lung cancer. After a courageous year of treatment, he died. But before his death, he praised the nurse and the other people who showed him tenderness, calling their small gestures of humanity "moments of exquisite compassion."

Schwartz said, "I realize in a high-volume setting, the high-pressure atmosphere tends to stifle a caregiver's inherent compassion and humanity. But the briefest pause in the frenetic pace can bring out the best in a caregiver and do much for a terrified patient....These acts of kindness...the simple touch from my caregiver...have made the unbearable bearable."

Days before his death, Schwartz gave an extraordinary gift back to medicine. He created the Kenneth B. Schwartz Center at Harvard University to promote a healthcare system that promotes compassion between patients and caregivers. With the center's support, more than a hundred hospitals are training more compassionate caregivers.

The simplest acts of love can make life not only bearable for others but beautiful. Small gestures are great peacework. Whether you work at a daycare center or a gas station or a large corporation, if you bring inner peace to others by serving them with kindness, you spread outer peace far beyond your act of service. "The only lasting security is found in love," Gandhi said.

Service to others also helps us feel we belong to something greater than ourselves. "Everybody can be great, because everybody can serve," Martin Luther King Jr. said. "You don't have to make your subject and your verb agree to serve. You don't have to know about Plato and Aristotle to serve. You don't have to know Einstein's theory of relativity to serve. You don't have to know the second theory of thermodynamics in physics to serve. You only need a heart full of grace. A soul generated by love."

Begin to bring more grace into each organization you touch. Senior executive Kenny Moore has made this his mission at KeySpan Energy, a New Jersey utility. A constant flow of simple acts of kindness, forgiveness, and love have helped ease tensions greatly at his 13,000-employee company, which has undergone mergers and other changes. A former Jesuit priest and huge-hearted man who has survived both cancer and a massive heart attack, Moore knows well the healing power of love. He tells his story in his book *The CEO and the Monk: One Company's Journey to Profit and Purpose.*

As KeySpan's ombudsman, Moore brings the message of love in lots of simple but creative ways. For instance, each Monday one year, Moore gave flowers anonymously to a different employee, with a note saying, "Never think your good deeds go unnoticed." These acts of anonymous agape create a ripple effect of good will in our workplaces, sparking others to serve with greater gratitude.

They also make us feel more content, empowered, and confident that we can make the world a better place. Caring for one another is as powerful and binding as any peace treaty.

If love is this powerful in our homes and workplaces, how do we move it center stage in our culture and world? How do we take the force of agape and apply it to regional and global fighting?

# Let Your Heart Lead You to Your Life's Work

Let your heart break wide open at the world's suffering. Let it break open not to amplify the pain but to see it from your heart and vow to ease that pain. Let your softer, more expansive heart grow so powerful it can even embrace and help heal the world's pain.

This is what happened to native African Sam Gbaydee Doe. When he saw the horror and ugliness of the fighting in Africa, he wept, Doe says. He wept because "I know deep in my heart we're not different. And we have the same capacity to love and to care for one another."

Doe allowed his heart to lead him to his work as peacemaker and co-founder of the West Africa Network for Peacebuilding, which helps child soldiers reintegrate into their communities after surviving war.

"During the civil war in Liberia, I met this child who was very close to death. He was just skin and bones and was lying close to a school. Something drew me to this boy, and I went over to him. I made some attempts to help him. I went and got some popcorn and tried to slip it into his mouth, hoping that would help to save his life.

"After about 20 minutes, he opened his eyes. He looked straight into my eyes. After a few seconds, he shook his head and then he closed his eyes. In about 30 minutes, he stopped breathing. I stooped over him and checked his pulse, but he died. And that changed my life. I began to ask myself, 'How many children, as a result of the madness of others, are dying and are being deprived of the joy of growing up as a child?"

That questioning led Doe to his current work transforming violence through greater humanity and tenderness.

# Look at People with Your Heart

Look with greater compassion at terrorists, angry people, the disenfranchised, the violent. Keep remembering what Doe says, that "Those who have perfected violence are saying, 'I'm hurt.' In their society they haven't found a way of articulating that hurt, of expressing it...So [violence] becomes the way people express their trauma, their experience of fear, their anger, and all of the pain that they have internalized."

He has seen despair and violence mushroom into war. He has seen what happens to young children's spirits when they are taken from their families, forced to take mind-numbing drugs, and sent into guerilla warfare. He has seen the aftermath of tens of thousands of people mutilated and killed by conflicts.

But, even after all Doe has seen, he still believes in the power and energy of love. If he can still believe in love, so can we.

This is what Doe wants us to remember about the force of love: "If there is a form of transformation where social environments, cultures, and value systems emphasize the value of love, the importance of love, the importance of communication, the importance of relationship, the importance of community, then I think there will be a reduction in violence.

"There is no environment that can help transform violence except an environment that is characterized by love, by tolerance, by absolute acceptance of the person....and beginning to see the God in that person."

Can we try to see the God in one another, even our enemies? Try with at least your silent thoughts to see the goodness, the essence, the God in others.

That ancient wisdom of the heart can help us "take an imaginative leap forward toward fresh and generous idealism for the sake of all humanity," says Nobel Peace Prize recipient Mairead Corrigan Maguire.

This is the new story. The world is still an exquisite, divine, luminous place. We hold immense power to make it even more beautiful. What we focus on, what we dream for the planet will spread across the earth. "I believe firmly that love is a transforming power that can lift a whole community to new horizons of fair play, good will, and justice," Martin Luther King Jr. said.

Are you investing in joy and beauty for yourself and those around you? Or do you ignore your heart and invest in warlike thoughts, behaviors, and drama?

These are questions we need to ask ourselves more than ever before because these are defining moments like none we've ever seen. With our individual lives and the life of the world in a state of evolution, we can choose our future. We can choose to be as powerful as we would like to be—at heart.

Let's choose love. Love is capable of ending any pain we're now in. Love can allow us all to go home, one small act at a time.

## Love Even When Others Urge You to Hate

When enough people love fiercely, it simply isn't possible for darkness, hate, or fear to exist. "Love must be at the forefront of our movement if it is to be a successful movement," King said. Instead, we've often misused our personal and political power by trying to influence people through coercion and negative force. We have neglected to draw on the forces of compassion and love to bring us together.

King saw this when some of his followers urged him to use the power of hatred, not compassion. Some members of King's church argued that he should take a militant approach. "A member of my church came to me one day and solemnly suggested that it would be to our advantage to 'kill off' eight or 10 white people. 'This is the only language these white folks will understand,' he said. 'If we fail to do this, they will think we're afraid. We must show them we're not afraid any longer.'"

But King continued to embrace love, saying love was "one of the most potent weapons available to the Negro in his struggle for freedom." King not only used love as a rallying cry but showed how to love. Love is simple but not always easy; King made it look both, even in the most horrific moments.

Martin Luther King Jr.'s story, Louise Diamond's story, the stories of Jesus, Buddha, Mohammed—they all show that love can move mountains. Love tells us we belong to one another. We are here for one another. It speaks to the tenderness in each of us that wants to know only love, not brutality.

Decades after King, Archbishop Tutu wanted to overcome the repressive policies of apartheid. He, too, knew that love could speak to the white politicians who resisted giving up their old ways. Again, facing a population of angry, vengeful people, Tutu warned black Africans not to resort to violence.

"Be nice to whites. They need you to rediscover their humanity," Tutu said often. He insisted that there was no limit to God's grace and that this force of loving grace alone could change the heart of the prime minister and other South African leaders.

At the same time, Nelson Mandela was meeting with Prime Minister F.W. DeKlerk and, as he did so, Mandela also vowed to bring his heart and love into those summit meetings.

The power of love as a force of reconciliation and healing was visible to the entire world during those epic times. Apartheid was eventually overcome.

We need more leaders like that right now. We can find them, elect them, become them. Why can't you and I be the leaders for love? What if we conducted ourselves as if love were the foundation of our culture?

Training grounds for terrorists have cropped up all over the world. Some people sign on to practice the power of hatred. But many more of us—millions of us—have been in deep, spiritual training for years. We are deploying the power of love.

# Lavish Love on Those Incapable of Loving

Peacemaking ultimately provides people with the opportunity to be what they were meant to be, allows them to share their highest light and love with the world. Some people, of course, have rarely, if ever, been given that opportunity. They've led traumatic lives in which their darkness has been nurtured and their humanity extinguished.

Sam Doe focuses on nurturing the light in child soldiers. He has seen those who lost arms and legs in fighting. He has seen child soldiers in Sierra Leone who had to shut down their hearts before they could even fight. "Some of these kids were university students; some of them came from communities where relatives and friends were there, people they shared their love and lives with some time back. And then I asked, 'At what point did they change?'"

Doe found out that children from Sierra Leone, to toughen up for war, would do horrific things, like gouge their faces with blades, then put cocaine on their wounds, and bandage them. "They use that to see people as less than human."

They express their fear, anger, and trauma in violent ways. Ultimately, that is why we have to create a society everywhere that promotes the tenderness and value of the human person, Doe says. We have to "lavish love on those incapable of loving."

Our fierce hearts can take us through the doorway of understanding to ensure that all the world's peoples, even those we currently brand our enemies, are safe, loved, and made whole. We have to love so much that we return love even to those who have hurt us.

Amber Amundson has done that. Her 28-year-old husband, Craig, was killed at the Pentagon, leaving her to raise their two children, 3 and 5. In spite of her loss, Amundson has continuously stood in love and focused her response to September 11 on love, understanding, and compassion. She has spoken out against the war against terrorism, fearing that the deaths of her husband and others September 11 "will be used to justify new violence against other innocent victims."

Beyond this public activism, Amundson has helped her children realize they can focus on peaceful responses to hateful actions. She wants them to understand that violence is never solved with more violence and that their father would only want them to love.

Acts of revenge only "mock Craig's vision of America as a peacemaker in the world community," Amundson says. She believes love can heal, and love can deepen understandings between people, even when they are deeply divided.

In fact, she believes Craig passed into heaven loving even the terrorists who brought about his death. This belief of hers has attracted sharp ridicule, even from her own family members. For months after Craig was killed, some dismissed Amundson as an overly emotional, irrational widow. Because she failed to call for revenge and refused to hate the terrorists responsible for Craig's death, they said she'd lost her mind.

Even Amundson's father, who wanted to rip out Osama bin Laden's heart, wished she would snap out of it and cry out for vengeance. But Amundson continues to call not for payback but for peace. Almost overnight, her powerful call has moved people all over the world and inspired them to work for peace.

One of the founders of the worldwide group Peaceful Tomorrows, she received continual supportive e-mails and phone messages from people everywhere. Her resolve to choose to stay in a place of peace and gratitude was inspired by Craig's own example, Amundson says.

Craig was a gentle man who loved nature, painting, and flowers. He was fully awake and recognized the beauty of life. "When I was pregnant with Elliott, we were reading *The Tao of Pooh*, and I said to him, 'This is amazing. You really remind me of Winnie the Pooh.' Craig was a very peaceful, gentle soul." So his wife is determined to display that same sense of peace and generosity, not only for herself, but also for their children.

"I am speaking out against the war because life is precious. Craig is gone, and seeing someone I loved in my life one day, vibrant and happy, and not the next, I realized how fragile and beautiful humanity is.

"We owe it to Craig and all the people who died, and their children and grandchildren, to find ways not to separate from one another but to connect and live together."

Losing her husband was the "deepest loss imaginable—he was everything I hope our world can become." But Amundson says it would be even more painful to succumb to vengeance. "It does not feel good to hate. It does not feel good to hurt others. It does not feel good to separate from the whole."

To her, the whole of life has taken on keener spiritual dimensions since Craig's sudden death, Amundson says. She now realizes that a conversation she and Craig once shared about mortality and the meaning of life may have been predestined.

"As Craig and I were planting flowers in our garden, he said he thought that people were like flowers, all wonderful and all part of the cycle of life and death. He said, 'Honey, do you really think that when some of us die, the Creator will say, 'You go to hell, and you go to heaven?' I actually think we are all like flowers, and when the flowers and we die, we all go back together into the cycle of life and death."

That conversation now gives her comfort. "Without that discussion, Craig's death would have been extremely confusing and scary for me. Now I can see that his death, like his birth, is beautiful. Two beautiful moments in his life that show how significant we all are."

Amundson feels that the purpose of Craig's death was to teach us all how to love better, even how to stop hating the terrorists of September 11. "I believe, in our passing, we are all equal. I had a level of reconciliation on the day Craig passed because I felt that he and the terrorist who drove his plane into the Pentagon were holding hands as they transcended this life.

"This is the image I see: Craig would have run to those other spirits who died with hatred in their hearts. He would have shared his peace with them. Craig would have said, 'You died with hatred. I don't want you to pass this way. Please know me. Please know love.'"

Amundson says she has no hatred for the terrorists who killed her husband, only sadness that they never felt the depths of love in this existence.

"I know hatred killed Craig, and I have made a promise that I will love, always love. I can't be part of hatred and anger. I will be an example to my children that love is always a better way."

There is no other way. Love is the only way. Love is our greatest power, our best defense, our truest security, and our ultimate homecoming.

As powerful as brilliant minds are, they alone cannot make peace. Without our immense hearts, too, the world will not be repaired. For peace to become the bedrock on which we rest, we have to reclaim our compassion.

"The truth is, what one really needs is not Nobel laureates but love," writes Jack Kornfield in *A Path with Heart*. "How do you think one gets to be a Nobel laureate? Wanting love, that's how. Wanting it so bad one works all the time and ends up a Nobel laureate. It's a consolation prize."

Even the Iraq War may be allowing us to find our hearts as never before. Activist Fleet Maull says, "This war may be part of a decline into darkness and the eventual destruction of civilization as we know it. On the other hand, it may be the...last throes of a dying system of nationalist and imperialist domination that will soon give way to a new era of global civil society based not on control and deterrence but on partnership, cooperation, sharing, interdependence, love, and compassion."

Love others well, and ask for love in return. That is how we secure the safe, peaceful world we desire. "There are people who will try to tell you that love is a luxury and that life in all its miraculous beauty is less urgent right now than the need to retaliate against the forces of evil. I am here to tell you that unless we respond with love, we will certainly hand evil its great and final victory," says Yael Lachman.

"Go out, right now, and plant yourself in the middle of that which you love most—the thing within you that is most alive. Now listen carefully, because as that love cracks your heart open, it will tell you exactly what this broken world needs from you. This is your holy work, and it cannot wait. Make it big this time. Make it so."

# WHAT MORE CAN YOU DO?

- **First, Be Gentle with Yourself**

We can extend tenderness to others only when we appreciate and are gentle with ourselves. When we can appreciate our own pain and loss, we can better empathize with others. Feed your own heart well. And from that fullness of heart, you can slowly tune into how you feel about your heart in relationship to others.

Look at how loving your self-talk is. What you say to yourself shapes your daily reality. How loving are you to yourself? We all have moments of gloom, but are your thoughts predominantly hopeful or negative?

- **Surround Yourself with What You Love**

Invite peace to take root in your heart and mind by loving well. Spend as much time as possible focusing on what you love and what gives you hope. Ponder what makes you absolutely energized with joy, whether it's a vase of yellow flowers, eating a great meal with friends and family, smelling the autumn leaves, hearing a colorful story from your favorite uncle, doing work you absolutely love, playing with a neighborhood child, or dancing to the full moon.

Instead of cursing what or whom you don't want in your life, practice focusing on what you desire. Even if you think you will never be friends with someone you have a conflict with, wish that person well anyway. Focus on the loving outcome you desire. You never know what can happen.

Spend time each day visualizing what you want in your life, from a happier relationship with your partner to a more meaningful job to a more loving home. Pull joyful experiences to yourself by directing your thoughts.

- **Let Love Root First in Your Home**

Believe in the absolute best for yourself and those you love. Start right where you are. "Peace and war begin at home," said Mother Teresa. "If we truly want peace in the world, let us begin by loving one another in our own families. If we want to spread joy, we need for every family to have joy."

Raise the joy in your home in any way possible. Play together more. Extinguish warlike ways. Talk over good food and soft candlelight. Turn on music and dance together. Grow a garden. Practice loving speech. Create holy moments in your home. Connect through shared experiences, favorite books, mountain hikes, the celebration of birthdays, new teeth, graduations, the funniest jokes.

Our hearts instinctively want to open, protect, and comfort, especially when times are troubled. Even when our days are so crazily busy we scarcely have time to breathe, much less try to connect with our "enemies," our hearts still gasp on some level to be more connected, more loving.

It's often the briefest, achingly simple moments—the smallest of pauses in the craziest of days—that bring us into kinship with one another and a blinding peace on the earth.

We wait and hunger for and mark the big, defining moments—the holidays, the anniversaries, the birthdays. But real magic happens when we stop breathlessly rushing toward those big, shining milestones and savor instead the millions of small moments right here, right now. Celebrate the first tulips, sunsets, new friends, old memories. Celebrate the gift and awe of being alive in a world thousands of people leave each day, often violently. Celebrate how very lucky you are. These are solid, substantial peace strategies.

## • Try Love to Ease Your Tensions

Could love be the balm for many of our messy, long-standing conflicts? How many of us have tried a pharmacy of self-help remedies to ease our broken relationships, only to fail?

Our own homes are the ideal training ground to practice using love to bring peace. Our relationships provide the chance to discover any explosiveness in ourselves, as well as our deep reservoirs of tenderness. Go to love to solve any conflicts. Even if others are going to war, try to be the one who holds and spreads kindness, affection, and calm within the family unit. Without it, nerves, relationships, trust fray and snap. Without love, war continues to break out constantly. Imbalances and wounds only get deeper. Without love, nothing is healed fully. Love is the first peace tool you want when your world at home is rocked by conflict. In your parenting, in your relationships, let your heart lead. Ask your heart to lead in your family decision making and conflict resolution. When you're in the heat of anger, breathe deeply to soften your heart. Speak lovingly and respectfully.

With an open heart, answers will come more easily. In your choosing to deploy the force of love, solutions and support will come more readily.

## • Serve Others with Love

Twenty million refugees have been forced by war to leave their homes. Many of us are also refugees from the lives we were meant to live, having fled them when the fighting became too intense. We can go home. We can go home if we resurrect our hearts and use them to achieve peace. Use acts of kindness and volunteerism to create the loving world home we all crave.

- ## Remember That Form Follows Thought

Keep thinking loving thoughts. Be mindful of how loving and conscious your thoughts are. What do you release into the world each day with your thoughts and actions? In what are you investing?

"While you may be very careful about what you pay for with your money, you are probably less careful about what you pay for with your attention," says author Alan Cohen. "In the long run, how you spend your attention affects your life far more profoundly that how you spend your money. Your attention is the strongest currency at your disposal. If you squander it, your life will result in one, big overdraft. If you invest it in things you value, you will collect interest big time—and be interested along the way."

If we think the world is uncaring, it will be so. Who wants more of that? We've seen it play out for too long. So believe the world is beautiful and loving, and it will follow that thought. Many people point to the late 1980s and early 1990s, when a feverish interest in spiritual matters and environmentalism surfaced. A critical mass of people awakened at this time to their deep need to shape a more humane world. They simply and powerfully yearned for a more loving place.

"The Berlin Wall came down; democracy triumphed with the people's overthrow of communist dictators; Nelson Mandela and F.W. DeKlerk were negotiating to end the violence in South Africa, and a new environmental awareness spread globally with Earth Day 1990," wrote Corinne McLaughlin and Gordon Davidson in their groundbreaking book *Spiritual Politics*. "It was as if things were suddenly coming together on the earth and humanity was being given an opportunity to make a major shift in consciousness, releasing the need for enemies and embodying a new healing Spirit." If we unify our will and intention, we can again bring about that shift in consciousness.

# *Eight*

# Forgiving the Unforgivable

Forgiveness has to be the most elusive peace broker of all. Even when we tell ourselves that forgiving is the right thing to do and that we'll feel better, we still can't give up the ghosts of our resentments. For years, often our whole lives, we clutch a handful of people whom we can't forgive. You can cram a lot of people into one, tight fist.

If asked, we might say, "Sure, the world needs more forgiveness. I'm all for it. Just not from me."

Let's face it: Forgiveness requires an agile surrender, a leap of faith, a spiritual grace we're often not willing to attempt. Taught to be resilient, tough, and in control, how can we trust that, if we let down our guard and let go of our grudges, we won't be hurt again?

Forgiveness is a setup, right? Who in the world wants to be that vulnerable?

The irony is that we've already set ourselves up for deep, raw pain if we haven't been able to forgive. Not forgiving drains our energy and blocks us from receiving all the goodness we might otherwise receive.

Unless we can stop clutching the moments when we were hurt or betrayed, we can't reach for juicy joy. We will never be at peace. "Resentment is like drinking poison and then hoping it will kill your enemies," Nelson Mandela says.

When we can't forgive but instead replay the traumas we have experienced over and over in our minds, we only retraumatize ourselves. We weaken ourselves. Who needs that?

Forgiveness, on the other hand, makes us strong. It empowers us. Forgiveness is a return to sanity. It's self-nurturing because it involves making the conscious choice to feel magnificent, not mangled.

But as you know, forgiveness, like grieving, is not a cakewalk. It may be the hardest thing you've ever done. Some of us can forgive almost instantly; some of us may take a lifetime. Forgiveness is often an ongoing, gradual process. It involves coming to better understand someone's past, values, weaknesses, and frailties. Forgiving may move us through deep anger, sorrow, and fear—emotions we've often tried to run from.

But once you learn ways to release that emotional baggage, forgiveness will get easier and easier. It's in the practice, like any skill you want to master. Try these forgiveness tools:

## Change the Situation or Change Your Thoughts

It sounds simple, but it's powerful. Noel Frederick McInnis once viewed himself as the product of a miserable childhood. "In my mind, unhappy childhood was a universal birth defect that everyone got afflicted with."

McInnis clung to his dismal memories of childhood until he was 40. Then one day in Chicago, while he was hitchhiking to Los Angeles to begin his ministerial studies, he had a sudden insight. "It was midnight as I stood in a light fog and heavy drizzle under the glaring lights of the interstate that passes through the south side of Chicago. The fog inside was even heavier. I was feeling cold, lonely, and paranoid."

As he stood there, lost in the fog, he was tempted to emulate Job, who cursed the day he was born. But for no fathomable reason, all of a sudden, a happy memory from his childhood surfaced in his head.

"I was astounded to discover that there actually was one! Next it occurred to me that if one such memory existed, there might be others. And sure enough, as soon as I had conceded the possibility, several more surfaced."

Neurologists have discovered that when we think one type of thought, the brain tends to yield up similar thoughts. If we think an ugly thought, the brain says, "Oh, here you go. I found a whole batch of ugly thoughts for you to look at."

If you're intent on forgiving, try to access healing, supportive thoughts. Sometimes, McInnis found, forgiveness is a "memory exchange." He realized that he had been unhappy for so long because he was holding onto—was still attached to—negative memories. Today he regards himself simply as a man who had a childhood. "Some of my childhood moments were happy; some of them were not."

When you can experience this level of release, you can detach physically, spiritually, and emotionally from the negative memories that have haunted you. By releasing yourself from draining memories, you retrieve your real, vibrant self.

You now have emotionally disconnected from the pain. That is huge. It can no longer affect you. Isn't that what you really want? Doesn't it feel much better to be free of all the pain you've carried for so long? "Unload your camel if you want to enter the Kingdom of Heaven," says Emmet Fox. There are myriad ways to unload your camel if you want to experience heaven right here, right now.

## Find Your Therapy, Healing & Forgiveness Rituals

Journaling helped Cathy Eldon, whose son, Dan, a journalist, was killed by terrorists while on assignment in Somalia. Cathy was eaten up with rage, pain, and guilt. "I even blamed myself. I wondered how it would be different if I had led a different life.

Would Dan have become a journalist if I had been different or if I hadn't left my husband years ago?"

Eldon reached for the only outlet she knew of to deal with her hatred for the men who killed her son and with the guilt inside her—her writing. "I could pour all my rage and pain into my journal, and that helped me transform my anger and the energy of loss into something good."

Through that process, Eldon learned how to forgive and look at her anger as a catalyst for something of greater purpose. She now writes books that help others channel their pain and loss so they don't become the source of more bitterness.

Forgiveness adds to the peace of the world in a powerful way. It frees us and the others involved from the trauma we clung to. "For both parties, forgiveness means the freedom again to be at peace inside their own skins and to be glad in each other's presence," says Frederick Buechner.

## Don't Wait for an Apology

With a forgiving heart, we can fully enjoy the magic of the present moment. It lets us absorb all the beauty life has to offer. We feel more trusting that the world is a wonderful place.

We often resist forgiving others because we think it serves the person who wounded us. We feel it gives them permission to treat others cruelly or somehow makes them dominant.

Forgiveness is about honoring and serving ourselves. It's about giving ourselves permission to be our best and highest selves. Life is too precious for us not to be our best selves. Knowing this, many of today's peacemakers say they had to learn how to forgive others and not wait for an apology.

To be his best self, Arun Gandhi had to give up hopes for an apology from the man who murdered his grandfather. "My mother, wife, and I went to visit with this man when he was released from prison, and we asked him, 'Why did you do it?' I wanted to see if he had any remorse.

"We ended up having several meetings with him and had a friendly dialogue—but he had no remorse. He still believed what he did was right. He wanted to be known as a hero."

Soon after that admission, Gandhi realized their conversations were over. "I said, 'I am now leaving you. I forgive you for what you did. It's not my burden to carry. It's your burden to carry in your life. I am discontinuing this dialogue now. You go your way, and I'll go mine.'"

Forgiveness is not about forgetting. You will never forget what happened. But you can liberate yourself to move on and embrace life. "You have to forgive and go on with your life. Being obsessed with anger only destroys us," Gandhi says.

## Now Forgive Yourself

When we remove the negative weight from our hearts—angry, unforgiving people have more heart disease—we free up an enormous amount of energy, which we can direct to being more joyous and compassionate.

Be compassionate with yourself about the times you have been unloving. Forgiving ourselves is the most difficult of all sometimes. Many people bury themselves under heavy shame. They add to the shame further with overeating, addictions, and other excesses.

Come back out, into the light. Be kind to yourself. Accept full responsibility for your choices. Own your behavior and choices; make no excuses or lies. Don't blame anyone else for provoking you or forcing you to do what you did. Make amends, as needed.

And then forgive yourself.

Only when we acknowledge what we've done with no "buts" or other qualifiers can we really begin to heal, says psychologist Marilyn Mason. "There's a mean, cruel part of each of us. It's our shadow self, and it's part of being human."

Stephen Levine shares this beautiful meditation for forgiving ourselves: "See yourself as if you were your only child; let yourself be embraced by this mercy and kindness. Let yourself be loved....How unkind we are to ourselves. How little mercy. Let it go. Allow yourself to embrace yourself with forgiveness. Let yourself be loved. Let yourself be love."

Forgiving ourselves is about realizing we weren't capable at one time of choosing a different response. But now we can make more positive choices. Forgiving another is about realizing that the person who hurt us wasn't capable of giving us what we needed—but we can give ourselves the loving, healing response we craved.

## Do Kind Acts for the Person You Want to Forgive

Sometimes acts of compassion will be the ultimate way to forgive and release anger because the higher energy of love in those acts transforms the denser energy of anger. The Desert Fathers said, "Malice will never drive out malice. But if someone does evil to you, you should do good to him, so that by your good work you may destroy his malice."

Dr. Dean Ornish, who has pioneered a holistic approach to healing heart disease, has often seen the power of compassionate acts to heal deep animosities.

His first research project included two heart patients. One was an elderly man who hated homosexuals; the other a young gay man. The two were paired in the project, and initially they were so angry at one another that Ornish had to stand between them so they wouldn't hit one another. Not surprisingly, each time they got angry, they experienced chest pains. "I thought this was the end of my very short research career," Ornish said.

Ornish then had the two men do small acts of kindness for one another, like helping with their laundry. By practicing forgiveness and kindness, even before they really felt it, they learned how to release their anger. They softened toward one another—and their heart pains disappeared.

Ornish says it's helpful to remind ourselves "that we are all in different stages of our growth and evolution. Someone who does not have a great capacity for intimacy or forgiveness now may develop it later." Altruistic acts may be healing in those moments because "giving to others with an open heart helps heal the isolation that appears to separate us from each other."

Choosing forgiveness when we have been hurt doesn't condone the wrongful actions. It is getting to the root of and trying to heal the source of the violence. Forgiveness involves seeing more deeply with the heart, seeing beyond the result to the cause.

## Try Understanding Why

It often helps to put yourself in the other person's shoes. Why did that individual lash out in anger? What could have led them to commit that act of violence? A growing groundswell of people is doing this kind of reconciliation.

In 2000, a 15-year-old boy and his eight-year-old accomplice broke into Temple Vietnam, a Buddhist temple in Roslindale, a working-class neighborhood of Boston. The boys, who lived in a rundown housing project nearby, used an ax from the temple tool shed to smash a statue of Avalokitesvara, the goddess of compassion. They also damaged the temple's front doors, windows, and a skylight.

Many people got livid and called for revenge. They wanted the full force of the law brought to bear against the boys. But members of the temple went to a place of peace. They concluded that the boys vandalized their temple not out of hatred but, randomly, out of their own suffering. The leadership of the temple met and calmly deliberated, making sure their emotions didn't cloud their judgment.

"The teaching of the Buddha is very clear. When you are angry, don't do or say anything out of that anger," said Chi Nguyen, spiritual leader of the temple.

The Buddhist notion of forgiveness is grounded in the idea that we are all connected. Because of that unity, the temple leaders concluded that calling for compassion, not revenge, was the wisest course. "We are not a separate entity from these boys," Nguyen said. "Everybody is like a cell in our own body. So if we hit them, it is like we are hitting our right hand with our left hand. The whole body hurts."

Nguyen and his congregation asked the police and prosecutors not to press charges. And that was just the first sign of how far their forgiveness stretched.

In an amazing spirit of compassion, they reached out to their community and neighbors. They felt they bore some responsibility for the destruction of their property because they had kept themselves cut off from their neighborhood. "We had never gotten to know our neighbors," said Bich Nguyen, temple president and Nguyen's wife. "The fact is, we did not reach out," she said, for fear that others would think they were proselytizing.

The temple scheduled a cleanup and cookout and invited neighbors, including the boys. "We believe small acts of kindness can have a big impact. You sow a small seed, and maybe it will grow into beautiful flowers," Nguyen said.

He wrote to Boston's mayor, and an outpouring of people from the mayor's office, the police department, the Healthy Roslindale Coalition, the local Catholic parish, and the area housing project all pitched in and helped plan the day. A flier printed in English, Vietnamese, Spanish, and Haitian Creole was distributed to neighbors.

Nguyen also met with the 15-year-old, Angelo. "I told him I was giving him something positive to do," Nguyen said. "I said, 'Your name is Angelo, so now I am promoting you to guardian angel of our temple.'"

Angelo came and worked the day of the cleanup. He realized that he never would have done what he did had he known the members of the temple.

Neighbors Together is now an annual cleanup in Roslindale that draws tenants from the project, private homeowners, members of Temple Vietnam, and many others. Something beautiful was born from something ugly.

# No Matter What, You Can Choose to Forgive

At seven, Tanemori's life was shattered when the United States dropped an atomic bomb on Hiroshima. The bomb, which killed his parents, most of his close relatives and virtually all of his friends, also wiped out his childhood.

Tanemori became a shell of a human being, filled with anger and hatred, glowing with white-hot determination that one day he would make the Americans pay. "To revenge I worked, by revenge I slept, for revenge I had to survive. Vengeance, my old friend, my old enemy, and my constant companion held me together."

When he was 18, Tanemori moved to the United States. For 40 years, he stoked his anger and waited to avenge the deaths in his family. One day, though, he had a mystical experience that changed everything. He was driving over the San Francisco Bay Bridge when he realized it was like the bridge he had built from his old life to his new one, and that bridge was being destroyed by his lust for revenge.

All of a sudden he felt a wide range of emotions, from hatred to love and compassion. And he saw a flash—a summer cloud reflecting the morning sun. Suddenly, the cloud brought a flashback of the mushroom cloud of radiation and death that had lit the night sky on August 6, 1945. Overcome with emotion, Tanemori pulled over to the side of the road and cried.

"How easy it is to return to Hiroshima," a voice said softly. Then he remembered a dream he'd had in a bomb shelter the night before the bomb dropped. In the dream, there was a fire, "a raging vortex" that changed into a white butterfly. When the fire had almost burned itself out, embers were still swirling in the air.

And as he watched, the embers changed into orange-and-black monarch butterflies.

"As they emerged, they created a symphony, an angelic chorus more beautiful than anything I had ever heard. Every fiber of my being began to sing with this glorious sound."

As he sat in his car, remembering some of the loving people he'd met since he lost his family, out of nowhere, a beautiful, white butterfly flew across the windshield. "It was just like the one I saw in my dream 40 years ago. It landed and stayed for some time, flapping its wings, surging with energy that I felt within. Then it soared into the blue yonder against the glittering of the midmorning sun."

The message of the dream and the butterfly suddenly made sense to him. The dream had been waiting, dormant, deep in his soul to bring about his inner transformation and bring about forgiveness, when the time was right.

All of Tanemori's anger and desire for vengeance suddenly "paled against the overwhelming love I felt. ...It seemed as if the energy of the butterfly removed the clay that blinded my eyes for four decades....I saw unmistakably and irrevocably that my enemies were not the Americans or Japanese society. The enemy was none other than myself."

Tanemori came to see that we can settle human conflicts and differences without resorting to violence, war, or endless cycles of revenge. We can enter into darkness and emerge again with the gift of new life.

Tanemori created the Silkworm Peace Institute, which is committed to promoting peace, healing, and cultural understanding in the United States and abroad. It showcases the experiences and journeys of individuals and groups who are on the path of forgiveness. "In looking at my life, I have come to understand that just as the butterfly creates something of beauty from its own sacrifice and transformation, so can we make a better world."

One forgiving heart at a time.

# WHAT MORE CAN YOU DO?

- ## Vow to Feel Wonderful

Are you ready to feel as wonderful as you were meant to? Are you ready to free your mind and heart? Do you want to take your energy to a higher, more nourishing place? As soon as you are ready to find the peace you lost when you were busy with the energy of hating, it can happen. As with all peacework, start small. Forgive the small things first. Remember how Colman McCarthy says we can begin by forgiving the person who almost sideswipes us while we're driving. Instead of flashing the one-finger salute, we can say, "Oh, I've done that before, too."

- ## Don't Wait for an Apology to Start Your Own Healing

Forgive someone "whose heart cannot yet see," says Thich Nhat Hanh. Our job isn't to get someone else to change and become a better person. Waiting for others to "get" what they've done and show remorse is a self-righteous choice. That choice harms only you, not the other person. It keeps you stuck in anger.

"When we do that, we end up clinging to anger for years, often at our own expense. We're leaving our well-being in the hands of someone else," says Mariah Burton Nelson, author of *The Unburdened Heart: Five Keys to Forgiveness and Freedom.* Our only job as peacemakers is to forgive and soften our hearts so they can shine a higher grace.

- ## Try Forgiveness Rituals

Try energy work, like reiki, journaling, sharing your story with a counselor, or chanting your pain. Find any strategy that helps you clear the bitterness that keeps you from having a loving, peaceful heart. Sometimes moving to a place of forgiveness requires something you've never tried before. Try "rewriting" the pain you experienced to remove any unhealed hatred, anger, or grief from yourself. Rewrite the story to finally let go.

If you don't stop replaying in your mind the terrible things that happened to you, how can you expect to release that terror from your soul? Like choosing not to respond to violence with more violence, we can choose not to keep playing those harmful thought tapes. We can choose freedom in the form of higher thoughts.

Close your eyes and visualize moments when you felt abandoned, betrayed, and hurt. Now visualize how you wish you had been treated. See those people treating you in a loving, kind, respectful manner. Visualize their giving you the response you wish they'd given you before.

Now try to forgive each of those people. Doing this out loud is especially powerful. "I now release this energy that no longer serves me. I am filled only with energy that serves my highest and best good."

## *Conclusion*
# BUILDING BELOVED COMMUNITIES

*A* s we now know, peace is not found in isolation. It's found inside us, expressed as us, with and through others. Peace is a living, vibrant presence that animates us, our partnerships, our friendships, our organizations, and our communities.

We are the peace. We anchor peace, here and now, in and through our very lives. "Heart, spark, spirit—whatever word you use for the mysterious force that animates us—its full potential cannot be realized in isolation," says *Soul of a Citizen* author Paul Loeb. We find peace in community with each other.

When King Hussein ruled Jordan and worked for peace in the Middle East, Queen Noor said, her husband believed that true peace was made between people. "By personal example, he inspired the different people of our region to understand what he felt so deeply; that real peace is made not only among governments but among peoples, that it is written not only on pieces of paper but must be enshrined in the hearts of those who live together side by side."

Communities—peaceful communities—are what allow us to thrive. And such beloved communities are our birthright, said Martin Luther King Jr.

Being in community helps us grow, allows us to be challenged, and gives us blessed opportunities to become better human beings. It gives us the gift of holding up one another's accomplishments and supporting one another in times of struggle, even when our values, beliefs, religions, and ethnicities vary widely.

Communities can bring out the best in us and allow us to do the same for others. Peace rises greatly whenever we find and form respectful communities. It's exciting to see the growing numbers of towns, support groups, Internet organizations, and coalitions—led by everyone from teenagers to senior citizens—forming peace-centered communities. They're helping one another ease their anger and pain by learning compassionate listening, laying down their weapons and fears, and creatively working out their differences.

Are you part of a peaceful community? Are you merely living in your city or town, or are you inhabiting it fully? Are you bringing it to life with your talents and resources? More than any people on earth, we Americans have the prosperity and well-being to ponder these questions.

We have the blessings, the health, and the resources to act for the good of everyone. We are blessed with so much abundance and so many gifts that we can become the new peacemakers, Desmond Tutu believes.

If peace can happen in South Africa, it can happen anywhere, he adds. It's time to believe that peace can come to our communities. It's time to believe, as Tutu does, that our enemies are our friends waiting to be made. It is time to believe that we are perfectly positioned to be the most generous people on earth and that any prosperity we have been given is no accident.

How do we begin to use our power to reach out to and bring peace to the rest of the world?

How do we start forming peace-first communities? The following are superb, inspiring examples:

Conclusion

# Hold a Vision for Peace in Your Community

Lucknow, India, is the home of City Montessori School, the largest private school in the world, with 25,000 students. The school's administrators, families, and students have made peace the centerpiece of their school community. Children at CMS learn to value world citizenship and religious tolerance. They practice meditation and being peace. They are guided to make peaceful choices by the philosophy "Every child is potentially the light of the world, as well as the cause of its darkness."

Parents are drawn to CMS because they know that, in an increasingly global world, their children's success will depend on how well they get along with children from other cultures, nationalities, and religions. Parents want their children to have a good education, but they also want them to have good morals, says Jagdish Gandhi, who founded CMS in 1959 with his wife, Bharti.

"The children here are inhaling a vision—a vision of globalism—so they can take up a position where they can change the world. I want our graduates to be self-motivating agents of social change, serving the best interests of the community and the world as a whole," Gandhi says.

This school community has already served the world well with its commitment to model peace in a religiously diverse city that is roughly 70 percent Hindu, 25 percent Muslim, and five percent Christian and Sikh, in a region where tensions can turn violent.

In 1992, widespread fighting broke out nearby after Hindu fanatics tried to demolish a mosque in Ayodhya, about 40 miles from Lucknow. More than 3,000 people were killed in the violence that followed.

CMS students, faculty, and parents knew that fighting easily could come to their city, so they decided to find a more creative solution. They decided to deploy peace; they believed they could

189

make a difference. That intention for peace set the stage for what unfolded.

Students took to the streets, hiring jeeps with loudspeakers. Driving through the city, they appealed directly to the people to refrain from violence. Their jeeps were followed by thousands of parents singing songs of peace and phrases like "The Name of God is both Hindu and Muslim."

"We had hundreds of children marching with a banner saying *God is one, and all mankind is one*," said Bharti Gandhi.

Because of CMS's leadership, the governor called a special meeting of all the city's religious heads. Every day, these leaders held public meetings with members of the community to discuss peace and harmony. Collectively, they created a zone of peace more powerful than the zone of war near them.

Lucknow escaped any serious disturbances, even though, all around it, Hindus killed Muslims and Muslims killed Hindus. Now, Lucknow's reputation as a peaceful city is known all over the world.

Peaceful communities like Lucknow become this powerful because they focus on what unites and connects us, not what separates us. They illustrate that our true power comes not from aggressively guarding what is ours but fiercely protecting the common good of all.

## Create Programs That Promote Tolerance

Use your imagination. Think out of the box. Gather your community leaders, educators, students, counselors, ministers, and business people, and brainstorm some ideas. Create regular forums and centers to air grievances, discuss issues, and explore peaceful solutions. Teach children and students how to express their truth without feeling that it's the only truth.

You don't need to create anything grand and imposing. Jagdish and Bharti Gandhi didn't set out to create the world's largest private school and have it listed in the Guinness Book of

World Records. Fresh out of college and newly married, Jagdish just knew that he wanted to serve humanity. He borrowed 300 rupees—less than $10—and rented a couple of rooms to start his school. His first class had only five students.

Start small to sow peace in your community. See what matters most to you. It might be to support the homeless. It might be to help children learn peace in schools. Maybe you can humanize your workplace so it's a kinder place for both employees and customers. Maybe you could write a weekly column for your local paper that explores acts of kindness.

The state of Minnesota launched the You're the One Who Can Make Peace campaign statewide in 1998. The campaign is built around a simple message: Every person is responsible for helping to reduce violence.

## Create or Join Peace Communities on the Internet

Many large, on-line communities dedicated to change have formed on the Internet, based on the idea that great things can grow from small ideas. After September 11, Eli Pariser, a 20-year-old college grad, was full of many emotions, like most of us. "I started getting very concerned that, with this terribly violent act of terrorism, we would play right into the hands of the perpetrators by responding and killing innocent civilians. I was sad for the victims and worried that more victims would follow and wondered, 'What can I do?' I felt helpless."

Searching his soul, Pariser tried to figure out a plan of action. "At the time, I was working as a Web IT manager at a nonprofit. I figured, 'OK, making a Web site is something I know how to do.'"

So he created a new Web site, part of which allowed people to contact congressional members and appeal for restraint so no more people would be put in danger. Pariser then aligned forces with David Pickering, who had started a petition against the war, which they posted together.

"The following Monday," Pariser says, "I got a call from my server administrator saying we had a problem with our Web site crashing because too many people were trying to access it. At that point, 10,000 were signing the petition in an afternoon."

After two weeks, more than 500,000 people from 192 countries had signed the petition. Media calls from reporters, from Holland to Romania, were streaming in. "I really think it was the right message at the right time. Sometimes something is on a lot of minds, and only one person needs to say it. I said it."

The Web site eventually became known as MoveOn.org and became one of the most influential voices for change in the world. It is also one of the most vibrant online communities, re-engaging people all over the world in public policy. MoveOn has more than two million registered members in the United States and 600,000 abroad—all because Pariser channeled his emotions into action.

"I don't think I'm particularly visionary or anything like that. I think I'm persistent. Persistent without being self-defeating, I guess. That can get you awfully far.

"Getting people involved in their government to reinvigorate democracy is terribly exciting. People come up to me pretty frequently and share how MoveOn has given them hope and gotten them back into politics or into politics for the first time. Those are my favorite stories—of people who have never cared about politics getting involved. It boils down to the saying, 'If not me, who? If not now, when?'"

If we want to reinvigorate our own communities—or create new forms of vibrant communities—we too must ask ourselves, "If not me, who? If not now, when?"

## Launch a New Community-wide Campaign

Sometimes, someone in a city or town can put out a call for peace activities and ideas and start a kind of contagious rally for peace in the community. Leaders in Peterborough, Canada, decided they wanted to increase the violence-prevention programs and responses in their community. So they launched the Peterborough Peace Builder Campaign, which called on residents to make promises of action to reduce violence and build a stronger community.

The stories of people making these "peace pledges" were posted on a community Web site, encouraging others to make their own commitments to peace.

The grassroots response was almost instantaneous. Faxes, e-mails, and peace pledges in support of the Peace Builder Campaign poured in.

One woman vowed to be more patient when she is kept waiting, especially in checkout lines. Barbara Earle, a city library employee, says she likes "the idea of making peace something we do." She promised to exercise more patience in public because she becomes annoyed standing in lines. "I've seen others do it, too. What we end up with is a few people radiating impatience and anger and some poor person getting the brunt of it."

Now when she's waiting in line, Earle focuses on "making it a quiet moment" and accepting that people are doing the best they can. "We can contribute to making our communities more peaceful places by helping others, not tolerating violence or aggression, or, I believe, by being a little nicer to each other."

The more this community of 70,000 consciously focused on peace, the more creative responses it got. Students and teachers responded by asking kindergarteners and first-graders questions like, "What does a peaceful community look like?" They encouraged the children to draw their visions of those peaceful communities. Others created multimedia presentations about peace and organized anti-bullying events. Students made peace pledges not to argue with siblings and to talk to their neighbors.

"It's really about little things. It's about watching your own behavior and modeling for others," said college student Emma Davies. "When I thought of peace before, it sounded like something on a world level. But it's really not. It's just about living your life well and encouraging this from others."

Davies decided to become part of the campaign because one has to change "the person within" to create a peaceful community, she says.

The Peterborough Peace Builder Campaign is a great example of what can happen when an entire community focuses on peace. It shows how much each one of us can do to change the tone of our own cities and towns. We create peace for ourselves right where we live.

"There is no 'they' that can take care of things," says Peter Pula, who has helped organize the campaign. "We have to actively choose the communities we want through individual choices, actions, and most importantly, through collaboration with those who share our interests."

## Start Where You Live and Work

If some of these community activities feel too ambitious, by all means don't tackle them. That would not be peaceful for you! Maybe you can use your work to create a more peaceful community, more easily.

For instance, Kathy Kenney, a yoga instructor and mother of three, believes our schools can be made more peaceful if we teach children how to steady their own minds. She regularly goes into schools in my community of Fort Collins, Colorado, to teach students yoga so they can calm and clear their minds.

Often during yoga sessions, students get so calm and quiet teachers are stunned, Kenney says. "Teachers will ask me, 'How do you get them to be so quiet?'"

Kenney's response? "I let them. I let them quiet their minds, and by letting them quiet their minds, the students come back to class more focused and more able to cooperate. They're able to look into their inner resources and respond more calmly."

Yoga, which means "to yoke" or "to unite," also helps students be kinder and more peaceful because they see they are part of one another, Kenney says. "Yoga is about opening the mind and heart and realizing our connection to each other. If I feel connected to everyone, why would I want to harm anyone?"

Self-esteem in students also rises because the practice gives them a sense of mastery, joy, and competence. They learn confidence, knowing they can control their own behavior. "Too often kids comply with a teacher, parent, or coach and focus, listen, and be quiet without really being intentional about it. Yoga allows kids to go inside and learn self-control. They know they are in charge of their own responses."

If yoga were a standard offering in our schools, we would see the violence in them plummet, Kenney believes. "I truly believe that, if each and every child grew up experiencing their sacred connection to life here on the planet and beyond, in knowing that truth about themselves, there would never be another Columbine."

## See the Genuine in People You Don't Trust

Like the students learning how to trust their own inner power, peaceful communities form when the people within them learn to trust. Sometimes this trust is tenuous at best, but more and more often, with the help of skilled peacemakers, once-bitter enemies are coming to terms with their pain and their barbaric cruelty to one another and building new bonds of trust. We can learn from and be inspired by their experiences.

In places like Bosnia, where once-neighbors and friends have harmed one another, it often takes every peace tool imaginable, from forgiveness to deep listening, for new bonds to form. It often takes skilled mediators to remind people of their basic goodness, which even the atrocities of war can't destroy.

Peacemaker Louise Diamond remembers the first group in Bosnia with whom she worked. "For most of them, it was the first time they had met with anyone from other groups since the war. It was very tense."

The group included a Muslim woman who had lost a son in the war. It also included a Serbian man who had been a soldier. "The woman had a great aversion to him. She saw him as the prototype or the stand-in for all Serbian soldiers."

The Muslim woman kept referring to the Serbian man as a soldier. And he kept responding, "No, I am an ex-soldier. I was once a poet."

At one point during the meeting, the man went into a corner and wrote a poem, which he later read out loud to the group. It expressed his unwillingness to participate in the war and how much he hated being a solider. "It was a powerful statement...his disavowing of that part of his life," Diamond says.

Once that Serbian man stood up and revealed his innate goodness, the emotions and climate in the room became dramatically more loving. From then on, the poet and the mother were consistently together, arm in arm. A new community began to spring from their friendship.

"Six months later, we met with many of the same people in the workshop and asked them what most stood out for them during the meeting," Diamond says. "An overwhelming number of people said the turning point for them was watching those two people."

When we believe that people in our midst still long for peace, after all that has happened in our lives, we can begin to see that peaceful communities are not only possible but are our destiny.

What do you believe about the people you've entered into community with, from your children's teachers and soccer coaches to members of your church? What do you see in the people in these communities?

Those people you spend time with are capable of greatness, just as you are. They are of you, part of you. Start seeing their souls. Know that together you can sustain and strengthen each other. Start standing up and showing your soul right where you are to create a community of peace.

Conclusion

# Open Yourself to Peaceful Opportunities Locally

Find ways to bridge differences, even in the smallest moments. Making this choice can be easy, gracious, even fun. All it requires is that you stay alert for opportunities to extend just a little beyond your own comfort level, says Elissa Tivona.

Actively look for peace partners, she urges. Join a dialogue group, get online, shake the hand of someone who practices a different faith, and be willing to see beyond the differences. One day, peace and reconciliation were as simple as displaying a message in her son's fifth-grade classroom, Tivona found. "One other mom and I were there to help the kids decorate for the holidays. As I knelt to pick up a wreath, the other woman knelt down beside me and pointed to the pin on my jacket that read *Stop Hate* in both English and Hebrew. Very quietly, she whispered, 'Tell me about this—your pin.'

"Her eyes filled with her heartbreak, and I knew instantly she was Palestinian. Among the many things we shared that morning—the morning that the Muslim and Jewish moms volunteered to tack up snowmen—was that I was the first Jewish person she had ever spoken to in her life. One small breakthrough, dispelling mythic distortions of so-called enemies."

# Work for the Good of All

Too often our towns are fractured by conflict because the interests of just a few hurt the majority. How much responsibility are you taking for the overall welfare of your community? Be excited about being part of the solution, not just part of the problem.

Again, we can learn much from people forced to patch together a new reality after overwhelming conflict. Dekha is an African peacemaker living in Wajir, a district in northeast Kenya. This area is a gathering place for shepherds and herders, who move their sheep, cattle, camels, and goats to wherever pasture and water can be found. Most Wajirians come from three long-disputing clans and some lesser tribes that all struggle to eke out a living in this parched land.

After a harsh drought in 1992, tensions and violence began to climb. Clan members stole land and livestock. Arson, rapes, looting, and murders increased. Refugees and weapons were coming across the border from war-torn Ethiopia and Somalia.

As their community's peace was shattered, some of the women in Wajir realized that they needed to do something. They saw that peace wouldn't just trickle down, like long-awaited rain soothing the cracked soil. It wouldn't come from a neighboring tribe or country. The women knew peace had to come from them.

"The problem had become explicitly ours. We women had no choice. If your house is on fire, what do you do? Sit and wait for someone else to extinguish it? No. You find a way to put the fire out," Dekha says.

One day, during a joyful wedding party, many of the women present couldn't help noticing that the merriment of the celebration clashed with the tensions outside. "We looked around and realized that a cross-section of all the clans attended the wedding, and we were feeling good. But outside this small compound, the happiness and the mixing was not there. So we discussed at length what was happening within our society."

The women kept discussing what they could do, and they decided to form Women for Peace. The organization started to take small steps to calm the tensions. Female members of warring tribes began sharing meals together. After one violent fight, women brought soap and household goods to the victims.

Soon the women approached the men—schoolboys to elders—and got them involved. Leaders of the major clans came together and formed committees to solve conflicts. A cease-fire among the clans was called in the fall of 1993. Then the communities began to stoke peace in their region even more fiercely.

Public meetings and discussions were held. Workshops explored the roots of conflict and how to calm them. People hosted peace festivals and days of peace.

But to make sure their hard-earned peace wasn't just a temporary reality, the Wajir Peace and Development Committee was created. It mobilized members of parliament, businessmen, religious leaders, NGO workers, security workers, women, and clan elders. Collectively, they created a rapid-response team of elders, religious leaders, and security officers that would move, as necessary, into any part of Wajir to defuse tensions and mediate conflicts.

The committee helps to "put off the fire before it spreads far," says Dekha.

We can see the power of intention in this community. We can see how their faith in peace was stronger than their faith in war.

And the people of Wajir decided they needed to go even further if they wanted to live in peace. They knew they must address the poverty that caused much of the tension. Steps were taken to ease the drought's impact and distribute food to those most in need.

Peace happened in Wajir when its people wanted it more than they wanted conflict. They longed for it so deeply it came to life. "Women for Peace was born out of necessity. We started with small initiatives that quickly launched into a highly organized movement. We knew that, though this was not simply a women's problem, we women could inspire positive change through nonviolence."

## Play for Peace

Michael Terrian, director of Play for Peace, an organization supported by the Dalai Lama, has also seen what happens when local community members believe they can inspire change through play. Play for Peace is a worldwide organization that helps people come together and play, connect, laugh, and find compassion and understanding.

Instead of going into war-ravaged areas and focusing on the problems, Play for Peace focuses on the solutions. "We look at daily living as a solution. We ask, 'What is the reality we want to create?' Then let's be that reality," Terrian says.

Too often, in high-conflict areas, people take a stand against something or choose sides in an issue. Play for Peace shows how peacemaking is about focusing on what you want to grow in your community, not what you want to eradicate. On the grassroots level, it uses community gatherings and play to help people rediscover the goodness in one another.

In India, Play for Peace has partnered with 250 existing community, Muslim, Hindu, and Christian organizations. The adults mentor teenagers, who learn ways to play, connect, resolve differences, and be together peacefully. The teenagers, in turn, gather younger children together and pass on what they've learned. Meals are shared; games are played; stories are told.

"The nature of play is cooperative and designed to build relationships. When you are playing with someone, there are no winners and no losers....Your ego is removed. Now you totally have relationships with other authentic human beings, losing all sense of time," Terrian says.

"When we are playing, laughing, touching, and connecting at a heart level—no longer frightened—we build relationships that allow us to see the sacredness of one another. We are no longer cut off from one another by thinking handed down over the years that others are 'mean,' 'dangerous,' and 'ugly.'"

After the play sessions, when stronger connections have been made, members of the groups step back, discuss what's happened and why they feel more like a community.

Play for Peace helps communities recreate and strengthen themselves, generation to generation. It has shown, over and over, the impressive power of community to heal misunderstandings and stop wars before they break out.

Conclusion

In 2001, tensions escalated between Muslims and Hindus in Hydrobad, India, where many people were passionate about building a Muslim mosque on the site of a Hindu temple. People in both the Muslim and Hindu communities were on edge.

One day, Hindus marched to the mosque to confront the Muslims. Expecting bloody battles, the police came with helmets, batons, tear gas, and shields.

But it turned out that hundreds of parents had formed Play for Peace groups earlier in the week. Knowing they were in a volatile situation, they had gone door to door and told their neighbors, "If you see any acts of violence, call us."

So when the situation at the mosque was on the verge of exploding, citizens involved with Play for Peace quickly assembled at the scene. "They stood in their saris and burkas, arm in arm and hand to hand, between the angry groups gathering and the police. They said, 'Just give us five minutes,'" Terrian says.

Their calm presence immediately stilled the air. The Muslims and Hindus went home without fighting. Many said they were impressed and inspired by the calm manner of their neighbors.

Terrian has seen the power of community ease similar conflicts in other regions, like South America, where guerilla leaders and citizens who fear them are coming together on common ground for the first time. "Rather than calling this a program for peace, it is about community. In a place of peace, community can be alive, colorful, joyous, and playful. It allows for infinite possibilities to occur," Terrian says.

## Be a Spark to Bring People Together

Our beloved communities are coming into focus more each day because conflict, unresolved and unhealed, is devastating. It keeps us from our deepest joy because, as the peacemakers in this book have shown, it hurts too deeply to be at war with those we are meant to protect and cherish. It's too painful to awake each morning, see the beautiful rays of light and realize that, once again, we are awakening to a world torn apart by wars of all kinds, nation against nation, neighbor against neighbor, partner against partner.

It is time now, more than ever before, to expand the definition of what it means to be human. We are evolving from a people often dominated by anger and violence to a people driven to make peace. And I am deeply grateful to the peacemakers featured in this book for showing us how we can participate in and fuel this evolution.

We need one another. We need the walls that separate us to come down. This is not a time to be cautious or hesitant. This is the time to speak out, act boldly, and look for opportunities to come together.

Wherever our hatred and mistrust separate us, we need to speak our truth about peace. We are the messengers, and if we want the message of peace to ring loudly, we have to deliver it.

Glenn Smiley was an advocate of nonviolence who went to prison for refusing to serve in World War II. He also worked with Martin Luther King Jr., beginning with the Montgomery bus boycott.

In the late 1960s, Smiley had a series of small strokes that affected his memory and speech. For 15 years, this man, who had spoken out his whole life for truth and justice, did not speak publicly.

Then one morning, Smiley woke up and was apparently normal. He went on to give another 103 major lectures before he died at 83 in 1993. After he reclaimed his voice, this is one thing Smiley felt compelled to share: "In a world of superpowers armed with unthinkable weapons, the search for alternative means of defense and changing the social structures has become an absolute necessity....You have to act on the convictions you have today, or you will never act at all."

If not now, when? If not you and me, who? It's time to find our voices, our will. It's time to act. When we find our voices and act in behalf of a more peaceful world, lo and behold, we find our beloved community.

That is what happened to Anne Benson of Minneapolis. When Wisconsin Senator Paul Wellstone was killed, his death "really made me think about the importance of acting on your values and trying to make a difference in the world," Benson says. Then as President Bush started the move toward war in Iraq, she started to reclaim her voice.

Benson participated in local peace rallies and marches and attended a major anti-war rally in Washington, D.C. Along the way, she met Rachel Goligoski, and they attended training through Friends for a Nonviolent World. The two women decided to gather all their neighbors together for a meeting.

"We hoped we could stop the war. We hoped we could educate people about the lies and distortions that were being used to promote this war. But mostly, we hoped to meet neighbors who shared our feelings about the war, so that we wouldn't feel so isolated by our anti-war sentiments."

The women booked a meeting room at the local library, delivered letters door to door, and expected a handful of people to show up. "We were quite surprised when 60 people showed up at the first meeting! The room was significantly overcrowded, and the librarian informed us that we'd have to reduce the group size to 20 because we were in violation of the fire code."

That was the beginning of Neighbors for Peace, which is a powerful example of the grassroots nature of the peace movement and peaceful communities. People everywhere are sensing a need to speak out, mobilize, come together, and anchor peace in their own towns.

Since then, Neighbors for Peace has organized educational events, vigils, and a major peace march in St. Paul, Minnesota, that drew 8,000 people. They've collected school supplies for Iraqi children and raised about $4,000 for Iraqi humanitarian aid at a Neighbors Lend a Hand benefit concert.

They also organized the Neighbors Carry It Forward concert on the anniversary of Paul and Sheila Wellstone's deaths. They hope to sponsor speakers and events that will stimulate productive dialogue among neighbors with differing views and opinions.

Yet beyond all the events and activities, Benson says the most important thing she's gained from Neighbors for Peace is "a significantly larger circle of friends." The group is really much more than a political organization, she says. "Our meetings have become gatherings of friends. It continually amazes me that, nine months ago, I didn't know anyone from the group. Now they are an all-important part of my life."

The community she has found in the group has also built her confidence and helped her reclaim her voice, Benson says. "In situations where, in the past, I might be reluctant to voice my opinion or take a leadership role, I now feel comfortable speaking out."

These times call us to find and raise our voices. Peace is not just the work of politicians, diplomats, mediators, and war-zone negotiators. It is our work. It is you and I using our hearts, our breath, our words, our actions, and our fierce convictions to anchor peace wherever we are.

Will we have peace in our lifetime? We can have it when we see ourselves in each other. When we see that we are one. How can we harm one another when we see we are of one body, mind, and soul?

When will we be at peace in our world family? When we stop resisting our differences. When we no longer use the richness of our diversity to tear our communities apart. We will have peace when we exult in and honor those differences, knowing they were created for our pleasure and perfection, says Desmond Tutu.

"We were meant to live in a delicate network of interdependence. We were made different so we could recognize our absolute need for one another....I need other human beings in order to be fully human….My humanity is caught up in your humanity."

Together, we celebrate our shared humanity. Together, we create peaceful homes, beloved communities.

In writing this book, I often saw that it was those who had lost their communities to war who were leading the way home to the peaceful communities for which we long. Often those who are working to reclaim their homelands can best help us reclaim our own humanity.

And this is why I have saved this shining story for last. It beautifully exhibits the peace principles woven throughout this book. It shows the power of compassionate listening, of setting the intention for peace. It models how to forgive and how to channel anger and pain into a greater good.

Twenty-one-year-old Kimmie Weeks lost his home in Liberia to war when he was 10. He has lived a nightmare most of us can't even begin to understand. Weeks almost died because of the war in Liberia. Now he lives with great joy, knowing he survived to be peace, to teach peace, to inspire others so they, too, can live peacefully.

Wise beyond his 21 years, Weeks is a highly respected peacemaker and humanitarian, supported by officials at the United Nations, UNICEF, and UNESCO, and by friends like Desmond Tutu. His story shows how aligning with the ways of peace brings amazing grace and guidance—and opens us up to the larger life we're destined to enjoy.

When Weeks was nine, living with his mother in Monrovia, Liberia's capital, war broke out between rebel factions and the oppressive government. At first there was jubilation, Weeks remembers.

"It was Christmas Eve, 1989, when the war was announced, and celebrations were held in the streets, with everyone dancing. I was with my mom, and we were all happy about it. We were told it would only take three days for the rebels to march to the capital. It would all be over in three days."

How often do we make the same error in judgment? How often have we thought our own wars would be quick, clean victories?

Liberia's national army kept holding off the rebels, who eventually started to "kill, burn, loot, rape people, and conscript children into their army," Weeks says. "Soon people realized this is no glorious revolution....We started seeing images of dead bodies on TV......Images of war were coming in, fear was building for us in the capital, and no one was dancing anymore."

By the time the fighting reached the capital, and Weeks's home, a year later, supermarkets and schools had closed down, most doctors had left the country, and anyone who had a visa, money, or contacts had fled. Because they lived near the government-run radio and TV station, Weeks and his mother were soon trapped in their home in one of the hottest battles of the war.

"All I knew about war and gunshots I had seen from watching GI Joe and Rambo on TV, but it was a whole other thing being there in my house, huddled in the corner, and hearing this constant barrage of gunfire and heavy artillery going *boom, boom, boom* all around you. What made it scary was you didn't know if one of those missiles would land on the house and blast it away. It was a very scary, scary thing."

A week after huddling in a corner of their house, crawling out only for brief periods when both sides would call for a cease-fire so they could reload, Weeks, his mother, an older cousin, and his cousin's girlfriend decided to abandon the house and try to find a safer area of the city. But government forces saw them walking away and started firing on them.

As they ran, Weeks remembers hearing the horrifying *swish, swish* of bullets around him. "It was a complete miracle no one got shot or hit. We ran for what seemed forever, jumping into a swamp, where we stayed for a night. Some people were living there for days. They figured if they were hiding there, even if a missile dropped, the swamp would swallow it. And no one would find us in the swamps."

Escaping that gunfire as a young boy was one of the first of many miracles that saved his life, Weeks says. But horribly, as they fled, they somehow got separated from Weeks's mother, who, they found out later, had sat on the ground as the bullets sprayed around her.

Weeks, his cousin, and his cousin's friend found shelter at the home of his old nursery-school teacher. Weeks knew that his mother was probably dead. "I am 10 years old, and all I'm thinking is that my mother is dead and all I have is my cousin."

And then things got even worse. One day, rebels came knocking at their door. "They were pretty terrifying because they were wearing dresses; some wore wigs, and they had strapped human tongues on strings of the people they had killed....You see this and you know this person is not stable. We walked out of the house, and we were completely petrified."

Amazingly, after the rebels interrogated them, Weeks, his cousin, and his friend were released. Again they started walking and walking, eventually joining a stream of thousands of displaced people walking along the main highways, looking for shelter. "We could barely see the road because it was literally covered with bullet shells."

Eventually they tried to find shelter at one of the universities, where people filled classrooms, bathrooms, any space in which they could sleep. But when Weeks and his cousin found no room, they turned around and started to walk away.

Then Weeks heard his name called. "I turned, and there is my mother, and she is screaming, and I am screaming, and we are running! It was a complete miracle."

After more than a month apart, with rebel and government forces destroying parts of their city, somehow they had found one another again. Weeks still finds their reunion amazing. "She could have gotten on a ship, gone to another campus, left a day later...."

After going back and forth behind rebel and government lines for shelter, almost getting shot, Weeks's mother had somehow found her way to the same campus her son had gone to. Weeks is convinced some greater, spiritual power was looking out for them both.

For the next year, Weeks and his mother lived with other families in the corner of a little classroom, eating rations the rebels gave them. "Sometimes we would just get a pinch of rice a day," he says. Thousands of people were crammed together, with no basic health services, sanitation, or medicine. Soon chicken pox, cholera, and other diseases broke out in the community.

Weeks got gravely ill with yellow jaundice and cholera. His mother prayed over him constantly, he remembers. But when he lapsed into unconsciousness and a pulse couldn't be found, it was assumed he had died. His mother was restrained as Weeks was carried to the shallow grave that had already been dug for him.

"Miraculously, my mom managed to break away from the two people holding her, and she rushed outside, and she grabbed me and she shook the life back into me. I wake up, and see her face all dirty with tears streaming down, and I wonder, 'What the heck has happened?'"

Weeks says support somehow kept coming to him and his mother. "We had no food or money, yet every single day, we got something to eat, a root or leaf, nothing extraordinary, but always something....My mother's prayers, my prayers, it seemed almost everyone in that place was praying...There was definitely a huge, guiding force I was absolutely grateful for."

So grateful that Weeks soon set the intention to become a peacemaker. He decided to work so children like him didn't have to go through war and suffering. The humanitarian relief from UNICEF, with its blankets, doctors, and grace, was burned into his mind. He resolved he would help heal conditions somehow, even if he didn't know where to start, Weeks remembers.

He set the intention to work for peace, beginning in his own neighborhood. "When we returned home, all the young people said, 'Let's start simple. We can do a cleanup campaign because our community is still littered with bodies and bullets... Let's clean up all the debris and make our community better.'"

From those beginnings, with rebel forces then controlling 95 percent of the country, Weeks's activism swelled. With some of his friends, he started advocacy groups to pressure the government to open schools and hospitals. He brought peace marches to the high school. He focused on children's rights.

"In 1996, I decided to focus on the child soldiers because there were children our age who had been fighting since 1990, when they were 10, and now at 16 all they knew was guns, survival, how to kill and terrorize. These were children who basically had their childhoods stripped away from them.

"We all basically lost a portion of our childhood, but for the child soldiers, there was a greater tearing apart. Some of these soldiers had a gun in one hand and a teddy bear in the other."

There were by then about six or seven rebel forces controlling the child soldiers. Weeks decided it was time to appeal to the rebel soldiers—and he was the one to do it. Amazingly, seeing how effective he and his friends had been already, UNICEF decided to support their efforts.

Again Weeks had to leave the relative safety of his home and meet with the rebels of the dresses, wigs, and tongue necklaces, and their generals. "At that point, I was definitely at risk, but we also had an awareness that we stood a chance of doing more good for more people. ...We ultimately had the recognition that, if we were to die, we would die trying to make our country better; we would die trying to help other children, and that was the courage we had.

"I'm not saying I wasn't scared talking to the rebel troops, because at any time they could have killed us, but the more we did, the more confident we became. Somehow, something was guiding us and protecting us and keeping us from harm's way."

At the same time, the international community was putting pressure on Liberia to free its child soldiers. But what tipped the balance, Weeks believes, was the children's mobilizing and speaking out. "I think that shocked the rebels into saying, 'Wow, if the children are organizing, there must be something terribly wrong with what we are doing.'"

The power of one person's holding the intention for peace again is a force beyond anything we can make rational sense of. Don't even try. That kind of soul force is immeasurable. As a messenger to the rebel forces, Weeks was victorious. All the child soldiers, the youngest six years old, were disarmed.

But in 1998, the government began to recruit the children once again and tried to keep its efforts secret. By that time, Weeks was 17—and even bolder. Though he couldn't believe the brutal practice was being resurrected, he decided to investigate for himself.

With his camera and tape recorder, Weeks went directly to the military base where the clandestine training was rumored to be happening. Sure enough, he saw about 500 children between 10 and 18 being trained, and he immediately notified the media and international community.

This time government officials retaliated and started to hunt for Weeks. Ironically, even though they'd assumed children could kill in the war, they didn't assume a teenager could be leading this revolution. They went looking for an *adult* named Kimmie Weeks, even asking Weeks himself at times if he knew where this man Kimmie Weeks was. "I would say, 'We don't know where Kimmie Weeks is, and we haven't seen him for a while.' But eventually they got smarter."

When government forces started monitoring his home and showing up at his school, Weeks knew his life was at stake. An embassy he declines to name helped him leave the country immediately, smuggling him out dressed as a traveling folk dancer. He left so abruptly he couldn't even say goodbye to his mother, whom he wasn't able to talk to for another four years.

# Conclusion

Weeks eventually gained political asylum in the United States. He is now enrolled at Amherst. He continues to serve as an international peacemaker and spokesperson for children's rights.

Though Weeks no longer lives in his native community, he is creating new ones that seed peace all over the world. His community is now the peace community.

He has founded numerous organizations, including Youth Action International, that help young people work for change. His organization Voice of the Future continues its relief efforts in Liberia and other war-torn African countries. It rebuilds playgrounds, sponsors peace rallies and summits, and organizes ongoing dialogues between rebel forces and leaders. It also sponsors radio programs in Liberia and Sierra Leone that call for reconciliation and peace.

Speaking to elementary-school students in America is now one of the most rewarding things he does because most children are eager to hear about other parts of the world and want to know they can help, Weeks says. "I tell them that we have tremendous power to bring change, more power than we realize. When I talk about my projects, I tell them they didn't happen because I was a genius....My best ideas often came randomly, like in the shower.

"But it's always about taking the first step....I am not able to do this just because I lived though a war...Anyone with a heart and compassion and who hears about what happens to others around the world should take up a cause. We should try to make someone else's life better because we've been blessed. Our blessings in this country are not just for ourselves but to give back to the world."

Being a peacemaker doesn't mean you have to start a sweeping new organization, unless that's what calls to you. It doesn't mean you have to enter a war zone and negotiate peace there, unless you know that's your destiny. Being a peacemaker means acting from your heart, right where you are.

"The simplest things can save lives...If everyone in America committed to doing one, small thing locally or internationally, the world would be a much better place," Weeks says. If we were to put together all those small things, we'd have "a million miles of change." A million miles of change—what a wonderful concept.

When you set your intention to be a person who holds steady, who seeks peace, you can heal war zones and mistrust and conflict, beginning with your peaceful, hopeful presence, as Weeks shows.

"We can use our consciousness and creativity to think ourselves out of war and domination," says Elissa Tivona.

We are all Kimmie Weeks, Martin Luther King Jr., Mahatma Gandhi, Jimmy Carter, Elissa Tivona, Natalie Wieseltier, Lech Walesa, Alina Pienkowska, and all the grand peacemakers featured in this book. And they are all of us. Our suffering is their suffering. Our dreams and longings are their dreams and longings. Their choices for peace can be our choices. We all can work for a brighter future laid on a million miles of change and supported by infinite guidance.

We make the difference. We are the peace. Yes, there can be peace in our lifetime. It has already begun in each one of us.

# ABOUT THE AUTHOR

Susan Skog is a nationally known author, writer, and acclaimed public speaker. She is also the author of *Radical Acts of Love: How Compassion is Transforming Our World*; *Depression: What Your Body's Trying to Tell You*; *ABCS for Living*; and *Embracing Our Essence: Spiritual Conversations with Prominent Women*.

*Radical Acts of Love* features dozens of examples of compassion-in-action in medicine, business, education, and throughout our culture. *Embracing Our Essence*, offering the spiritual stories of women such as Jane Goodall, Drs. Christiane Northrup and Elisabeth Kubler-Ross, Naomi Judd, Betty and Susan Ford, and others, struck such a chord it was developed into a series of national conferences in California, Washington, D.C., and Colorado.

Susan has written about health, science, spirituality, and the environment for many of the nation's leading magazines, from *Science* to *Prevention*.

She presents at corporate, medical, government, educational, religious, and nonprofit organizations.

Susan lives in Fort Collins, Colorado with her husband and two sons.

# SHARE YOUR PEACEMAKING STORIES

Susan would enjoy hearing how you have created peace in your world. Share your thoughts, suggestions, and stories with her via e-mail: susan@susanskog.com

To order a copy of *Peace In Our Lifetime*, or to read more about the author and upcoming events, check out her website: http://www.susanskog.com.